The *Cathach* of Colum Cille

An introduction

by

Michael Herity

and

Aidan Breen

Folio 21r of the *Cathach* showing initial *M* and beginning of Psalm 56.

The *Cathach* of Colum Cille

An introduction

by

Michael Herity

and

Aidan Breen

Royal Irish Academy

2002

First published in 2002
by the Royal Irish Academy
19 Dawson Street
Dublin 2
Ireland
www.ria.ie

British Library Cataloguing-in-Publication Data
A catalogue record for this publication is available from the British Library.
ISBN 1-874045-92-5 (with CD-ROM)
1-874045-97-6 (without CD-ROM)

Design and layout by Martello Media Ltd, Dublin
Printed in Ireland by ColourBooks Ltd, Dublin

Contents

Acknowledgements

The Royal Irish Academy wishes to acknowledge a substantial anonymous donation without which the publication of the *Cathach* CD-ROM and booklet would not have been possible.

The Academy's Dictionary of Medieval Latin from Celtic Sources project, whose staff (especially Anthony Harvey, Christopher Sweeney and Angela Malthouse) prepared the digital edition of H.J. Lawlor's transcription of the *Cathach* manuscript for the CD-ROM, made a significant contribution to the project.

The assistance of the Academy's library staff and the advice of the Librarian, Siobhán O'Rafferty, are gratefully acknowledged. Thanks are also due to David Cooper of Digital Lightforms Ltd, Oxfordshire, for assistance with the project.

Mrs Harriet Sheehy kindly gave permission for digital reproduction of extracts from Maurice Sheehy's work on the Springmount Bog wax tablets.

The authors of the booklet wish to thank F.J. Byrne, Anthony Cains, Martin McNamara and Timothy O'Neill for their contributions towards the research on the manuscript. The contribution of Marcus Redmond, who acted as research assistant to Professor Michael Herity, is also gratefully acknowledged.

Permission to reproduce illustrations in which copyright is held by persons or institutions other than the Royal Irish Academy is gratefully acknowledged.

Image of Colum Cille, fol. iii v of Bodleian Library MS Rawl. B. 514 (Maghnus Ó Domhnaill's sixteenth-century Life of Colum Cille). (© Bodleian Library, University of Oxford, 2002)

Introduction

The *Cathach* is a manuscript of the Psalms in a relatively pure Gallican version of St Jerome's Latin Vulgate. The earliest extant Irish illuminated manuscript, it has been dated to *c.* AD 600 and is traditionally regarded as written by Colum Cille (Alexander 1978, 28–9). With its *cumhdach* or metal shrine, it was placed in in the care of the Royal Irish Academy in 1843 by the O'Donel family of Newport, County Mayo, who brought it back to Ireland, probably from Flanders (modern Belgium), in the early nineteenth century. To our knowledge, it is the only surviving Irish psalter for which a metal book-shrine was made.[1]

Colum Cille (521–97) was born at Gartan, County Donegal, according to his twelfth-century Irish Life (Herbert 1988, 275 n. 173). His father was Fedelmith, grandson of Conall, the eponymous ancestor of the kings of Tír Conaill; his mother was Eithne, who was of royal Leinster ancestry according to tenth-century sources (Ó Riain 1985, 76). He was fostered by a priest called Cruithnechán, studied as a deacon under Gemmán the Master in Leinster, later with Bishop Finnian, probably Finnian of Mag Bile (Moville, County Down), who died in 579, and, according to his Irish Life, with Mo Bí at Glasnevin.[2] Maghnus Ó Domhnaill, Lord of Tír Conaill from 1537 to 1555, related that Colum Cille spent some time as a hermit at Glend Colaim Cilli (Gleann Choluim Cille) in south-west County Donegal, where there are typical remains of an appropriately early date at the west end of the valley (Herity 1989, 95–106, 119–23). Colum Cille founded the monasteries of Durrow, Kilmore—the latter correctly identified by Reeves (1857, 173–4) as Kilmore, County Cavan—and Iona (Í Coluim Chille) in Scotland. Derry (Herbert 1988, 31) was founded or refounded, possibly in Colum Cille's lifetime, by his cousin Fiachra mac Ciaráin, who died in 620. The Columban federation later included Lambay (founded in 635), Drumcliff, Swords, Moone

---

[1] The scope of this booklet, which focuses on the *Cathach* manuscript, does not allow for a full discussion of its *cumhdach*, or shrine. A full description by E.C.R. Armstrong (1916), however, forms Appendix I of H.J. Lawlor's (1916) extensive essay on the *Cathach*.

[2] A list of Irish placenames mentioned in this booklet, with the counties in which they are located, can be found in Appendix 1.

and many other churches in Ireland as well as those of the *paruchia* in Scotland and Northumbria. After the Viking devastation of Iona, a *nova civitas* was founded at Kells in 807. The Columban church in Scotland likewise received a new metropolis at Dunkeld. By the twelfth century Derry had replaced Kells as the head of the *paruchia* (Herbert 1988, 113–23). The Annals of Ulster (AU), based on an early Iona chronicle and later continued at Armagh, were being redacted at Derry towards the end of the twelfth century or possibly earlier. From the tenth century until the beginning of the thirteenth century attempts were made from time to time to revive the unity of the Scottish and Irish federation under Iona.

A legend first attested in the late Middle Ages states that on a visit to St Finnian of Druim Fhinn (place unidentified), perhaps Bishop Finnian of Moville, who is credited with bringing the 'complete Gospels in a single volume' (probably the Vulgate) to Ireland, Colum Cille discovered a book and secretly made a copy of it. Maghnus Ó Domhnaill identified this copy with the *Cathach*. Finnian claimed that the copy rightfully belonged to him and referred the matter to Diarmait mac Cerbaill, King of Tara. The king's judgment, recorded by Ó Domhnaill (O'Kelleher and Schoepperle 1918, §168), has been cited as one of the oldest references to the idea of copyright (Fig. 1):

> 'le gach boin a boinín' .i. a laogh 7 'le gach
> lebhur a leabrán'
> (This may be translated as 'To every cow her
> calf, so to every book its copy'.)

According to the legend, this led to the battle of Cúl Drebene, probably fought at modern Cooldrumman, 3km north of Drumcliff, opposite Ben Bulben in County Sligo, where an alliance of northern rulers that included Colum Cille's uncle and first cousin defeated Diarmait mac Cerbaill in 561. The early eighth-century Iona annals (AU) record that the battle was won *per orationes Coluim Cille*, through the prayers of Colum Cille, but say nothing as to its cause, nor do they ascribe any blame to the saint. Colum Cille's biographer Adomnán, writing about 700, merely refers to the battle as having occurred two years before Colum Cille's exile (Anderson 1991, 30–31). Maghnus Ó Domhnaill, writing of the Battle of Cúl Drebene in his Life of

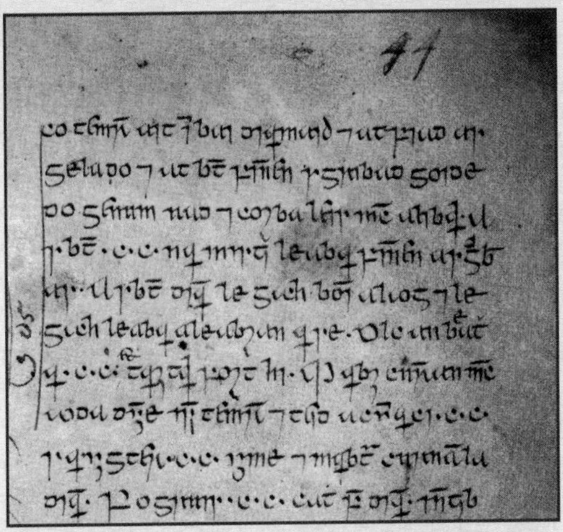

Fig. 1—Extract from RIA MS 24.P.25 (*Leabhar Chlainne Suibhne*, sixteenth century), fol. 44r, citing Diarmait mac Cerbaill's copyright ruling on the *Cathach*. (© Royal Irish Academy)

Colum Cille (O'Kelleher and Schoepperle 1918, §178; Lacey 1998, 100) at his castle in Lifford in 1532, explained the name *Cathach* (Battler or Champion) as follows:

> An Cathuch, imorro, ainm an leabhuir sin
> triasa tugadh an cath, as é is airdmhind do
> C.C. a crich Cineoil Conaill Gulban. Agus ata
> sé cumhdaigthe d'airged fa ór, 7 ni dleghur a
> fhoscludh. Agus da cuirther tri huaire desiul a
> timchell sluaigh Cineoil Conaill é, ag dul
> docum cat[h]a doib, is dual co ticfadh slan fa
> buaidh.

> (The Cathach, moreover, is the name of the
> book which caused that battle. It is the chief
> relic of Colum Cille in the territory of Cinél
> Conaill Gulban. And it is enshrined in a silver
> gilt box which it is not lawful to open. And
> whenever it be carried three times, turning
> towards the right, around the army of the
> Cinél Conaill when they are going into battle,
> the army usually comes back victorious.)
> (Transl. courtesy of F.J. Byrne)

The twelfth-century Latin Life of Mo Laisse of Devenish (i.e. Devenish Island) (Plummer 1910, vol. 2, 139) asserts that in view of the large numbers of men killed in the battle, the penance imposed by Mó Laisse on Colum Cille was exile. He left Ireland for Iona with twelve followers in 563 and died there on 9 June 597.[3] From Iona he founded the Hebridean island monasteries of Tiree and Hinba, the latter of which can most plausibly be identified with Canna, where there are important early Christian slabs and crosses (Campbell 1986, 5–6). It was from Iona that the Northumbrian mission was begun by Aidan with the foundation of Lindisfarne in 635. Colum Cille is credited with writing the *Altus Prosator*, a Latin poem of 23 six-line stanzas. At his death, Dallán Forgaill, 'ardollom Hérend' (Chief Poet of Ireland), composed the obscure *Amra Choluimb Chille*, an elegy of 183 lines, in which there is reference to his learning and to his interest in the Psalms:

> Gáis gluassa glé.
> Glinnsius salmu,
> sluinnsius léig libru,
> libuir ut car Cassion.

> (By his wisdom he made glosses clear.
> He fixed the Psalms,
> he made known the Books of Law,
> those books Cassian loved.) (Clancy and
> Márkus 1995, 106–8).

Adomnán's Life records several anecdotes about books and the writing of them on Iona. The saint wrote in a little hut made of wooden planks using an inkhorn (Book I, 19); on one occasion he wrote in the doorway of the hut (Book II, 16). On the day before he died he sat in his hut transcribing the psalter for the last time, stopping at the thirty-third Psalm with the famous phrase

---

[3] Dan Mc Carthy (2001) has argued that the Clonmacnoise set of annals has an internally consistent chronology that is at variance with that of the Annals of Ulster (AU) and has suggested that the death of Colum Cille took place in 593, not 597. However, the evidence of Adomnán, Bede and the majority of the Irish annals points to Sunday, 9 June 597, as the date of his death.

'Here, at the end of the page, I must stop. Let Baithene write what follows' (Book III, 23). Psalters were corrected by two pairs of eyes (Book I, 23). The account of two miracles records that books were carried from place to place in leather satchels (Book II, 8). That they were enshrined as early as Adomnán's time is suggested by the story in the same chapter of Book II. (For these and other events in the life of Colum Cille, see Reeves 1857; Anderson and Anderson 1961; Anderson 1991; Smyth 1984, 84–115; Herbert 1988; Sharpe 1995.)

When the shrine of the *Cathach* was opened by Sir William Betham, Deputy Ulster King of Arms, in 1813, he found only 58 vellum membranes of the psalter remaining, representing Psalms 30:10 to 105:13 (Betham 1826, 110–11; Lawlor 1916, 245).[4] The late Roger Powell, who rebound the manuscript in 1980, deduced from the pricking and ruling (Fig. 2) that it was bound in ten-leaf quinions, gatherings of five conjoint bifolia making twenty pages, of which five complete quinions and the greater portion of a sixth have survived.[5] Each gathering appears to have been sewn with a thread passing through three widely separated holes in the spine; Betham (1826, 110) noted that 'the sewing had almost entirely disappeared' when he first saw the manuscript. This arrangement in quinions conforms to a practice widespread, if not universal, in insular manuscripts as late at least as the Book of Armagh, written in 807. A lost eighth-century manuscript containing Old Irish saga material, the *Cín Drummo Snechtai* (of Dromsnat in County Monaghan), derived its name (Irish *cín*, from quinion) from this tradition of book-making.

The manuscript is written in a book-hand composed of confident, round letters with bold wedge serifs on the upright strokes, 'a deliberate creation out of elements of the several scripts inherited from antiquity which the earliest missionaries had brought with them' (Bieler 1963, 17). Lowe's statement that it represents 'the pure milk of Irish calligraphy' (CLA[2], xvi), is

---

[4] Psalm numbers referred to in this booklet and on the *Cathach* CD-ROM follow the Vulgate numbering, which differs slightly between Psalms 9 and 147 from that in the Authorised or King James Bible, which follows the Hebrew numbering.

[5] An extract from Roger Powell's report of 1981 on the repair and rebinding of the *Cathach*, with illustrations of the probable gatherings of the folios, is printed in Appendix 2.

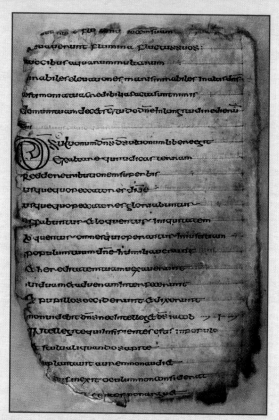

Fig. 2—Fol. 49v of the *Cathach*: a vertical row of pricking is visible at the ends of the ruled lines on the right-hand side of the folio.

often quoted; he allowed that a date as early as the time of Colum Cille is 'palaeographically possible' (CLA[2], 41). The psalms are written in brown or black ink, identified as gall, and are arranged on the page *per cola et commata* (by phrases and clauses) to facilitate reading or chanting aloud. Above each psalm is a heading written in orange in a space left for it by the scribe.

Lawlor (1916, 247–50) deduced that the minimum size of the pages was 235mm by 155mm, each pricked and ruled to take 25 lines of writing. He counted nearly 250 textual errors, most of them due to carelessness. Of 48 cases where one or more letters of a word is omitted, only 9 are corrected; over 70 corrections are made by erasure of one or more letters. He inferred that the insertion of superfluous letters, the copyist's most frequent error, was almost always detected and set right, while the omission of letters, to which he was also prone, was rarely detected. He observed that a large proportion of the corrections were made *currente calamo*, in the course of transcription, and that the manuscript was probably not compared with the exemplar after it was completed. Lawlor (1916, 250) concluded that the scribe was 'a penman of more than average excellence, who could not write rapidly but who was working at unusually high pressure when he made this transcript'.

Timothy O'Neill, a professional calligrapher, has observed (pers. comm.) that the scribe of the *Cathach* used an edged rather than a pointed quill, holding this at a fairly flat angle to the horizontal. This produced thick downstrokes and thin horizontals. The letters of the book-hand of the *Cathach* are formed by a sequence of strokes, left to right, top to bottom. Uncial (majuscule) *S* is formed of three strokes made with the pen held horizontally; *O* of two vertical strokes. The wedge serifs at the head of the verticals require an extra stroke each time and are not a feature of cursive writing, which is often characterised by signs of haste. This formal book-hand required, in O'Neill's view, a competent scribe writing in a controlled hand, fluently, without haste.

Each psalm commences with a decorative initial letter followed by a diminishing series of letters that merge into normal script (Nordenfalk 1947, 154). The initial, created by a thick black line on the vellum, is often surrounded by dotting in orange minium and has some elements filled with white lead tinged pink with madder, occasionally tinged with orange; Henry (1965, 61) noted the apposition between flat tint and dots, and the sharp definition of the lines. Commenting on the sensitivity of the artist to 'the subtle tracery of a pattern or to the sharpness of a line', she compared their attractive hesitancy to the art found on early pillars of stone. She observed that there may have been a decorated first page, now missing, which 'would have been invaluable for our knowledge of Irish illumination'. She considered that the manuscript, written well before the development of Northumbrian scriptoria, represents 'an essential landmark in the history of insular illumination'.

Provenance of the *Cathach* in the medieval period and later

The *Cathach* psalter was probably kept in a *tiag*, or leather satchel, during the early centuries of its existence. It is unlikely that the manuscript would have survived to the eleventh century, when its *cumhdach* or metal shrine is believed to have been made, without the intervention of hereditary keepers or the protection of a monastic milieu guaranteed by its traditional ascription to Colum Cille.

The eponymous ancestor of the Ó Domhnaill dynasty that ruled Tír Conaill from 1200 until 1608 was Domnall, who died in 965 (AU), and whose father Éicnechán (died 906) and grandfather Dálach (died 870) were kings of Cenél Conaill. Domnall claimed descent from the fifth-century Conall, son of Niall Noígiallach (Niall of the Nine Hostages) and ancestor of Colum Cille and his successors, the abbots of Iona.[6] Dálach was of the Cenél Lugdech sept, whose home territory included the Columban sites of Gartan and Kilmacrenan. Domnall's son Conchobar is styled king of Loch Beagh at his death in 1005. In 1129 (AU; 1130 AI) Áed Ua Domnaill was burnt to death in the church of Colum Cille at Kilmacrenan: he was son of the Cathbarr Ua Domnaill who enshrined the *Cathach* and who died as king of Cenél Lugdech in 1106.

Cathbarr Ua Domnaill was son of Gilla Críst, son of Cathbarr, son of Domnall, and he was killed by his great-nephew, the son of Conn Ua Domnaill, in 1038 (AU). This son of Conn, son of Cathbarr, may have been the Tadc mac Cuinn from whom the medieval O'Donnells descended; their claim to include the second Cathbarr, son of Gilla Críst, in their ancestry is found only in a relatively late source compiled in the reign of the great Aodh Dubh Ó Domhnaill (1505–37), father of the Maghnus Ó Domhnaill who wrote the Irish Life of Colum Cille in 1532 and who was himself to rule Tír Conaill from 1537 until his deposition by his son An Calbhach in 1555 (Maghnus died on 9 February 1566).

---

[6] The Ó Domhnaill family name is hereafter referred to, at different historical periods and in variant spellings, as Ua/Uí Dom[h]naill, Ó Domhnaill or (anglicised) O'Don[n]el[l].

It is most probable that the enshrinement of the *Cathach* in a metal box (Fig. 3) took place in 1090, the year in which, according to the Clonmacnoise Annals of Tigernach (AT), Óengus Ua Domnalláin brought the relics of Colum Cille from the north:

> Minda Colaim Chille .i. Clog na Righ 7 an
> Chuillebaigh 7 in dá Sosscéla do tabairt a Tír
> Conaill 7 .uíí. fichit uínge d'airged 7
> Aenghus. H. Domnallan is se dos·fuc atuaidh.

> (The relics of Colum Cille, i.e. the Bell of the
> Kings and the Cuilebad [Flabellum] and the
> two Gospels brought from Tír Conaill, and
> seven score ounces of silver; and it was
> Óengus Ua Domnalláin who brought them
> from the north.) (trans. courtesy of F.J. Byrne)

Fig. 3—Shrine of the *Cathach*: the gilt silver panel in the centre of the side of the box is part of the original eleventh-century work and features interlaced animals in the Hiberno-Norse *Ringerike* style. The lid was refurbished at a later date. (© National Museum of Ireland)

Ó Floinn (1995, 122) has suggested, following Herbert (1988, 93), that the *Cathach* was one of the 'two Gospels' referred to.

In a charter in the Book of Kells that can be dated to between 1076 and 1080, Máel Sechnaill mac Conchobair Ua Maíl Shechnaill and the coarb of Colum Cille, Domnall mac Robartaig (died 1098), granted the hermitage of Dísert Coluim Chille at Kells to God and to 'pious exiles'. In another charter, which cannot be later than 1094, Óengus Ua Domnalláin appears as confessor (*anmchara*) of Kells and also coarb of Dísert Coluim Chille, but Ferdomnach Ua Clucáin (died 1114) is coarb of Colum Cille, implying that Domnall mac Robartaig had retired from that position (Mac Niocaill 1990, 155–7). Mac Robartaig had succeeded Gilla Críst Ua Maíl Doraid, abbot of Iona, as coarb of Colum Cille in or after 1062.

The bringing of the relics from the North in 1090 suggests a deliberate policy on the part of Kells to assert its primacy over the Columban community in Ireland rather than the mere presence there of the skilled craftsman Sitric, son of Mac Áeda, whose name is inscribed on the *cumhdach*. It has been remarked that the terms of the inscription are unusual in that two patrons of the work are named. In the reading given here, the positions of rivets are marked by asterisks. Following established conventions, missing letters are given in square brackets and incomplete letters shown with a dot underneath:

> [*O]R*[O]IT DO [C]H[AT]HB*ARR UA
> D[*O]M[*NA]ILL LASINDERN[*A]D IN
> CUMTAOH[*S]A |
> 7 D*O SITT*RIUC MAC M*EIC A*EDA
> DO*RIGN[E] 7 [DO DO]M*N[ALL] M[A]C
> R[*OBA] |*
> RTAIG DO COMAR[*B]A CENANSA
> LASI[N*]DERNAD*

> (A prayer for Cathbarr Ua Domnaill who had
> this shrine made and for Sitric son of Mac
> Áeda who made [it] and for Domnall Mac
> Robartaig the coarb of Kells who had it
> made.) (trans. courtesy of F.J. Byrne)

The enshrinement may equally have been an assertion of the legitimacy of Cathbarr's claim to kingship, as the chief dynastic families of Tír Conaill from the tenth century to the end of the twelfth century were Ua Canannáin and Ua Maíl Doraid, based in the south of the territory (Gillespie 1995, 794–6, 813–14). Another battle-relic of Colum Cille's, his *cochall*, or cowl, is specifically associated in sources of the eleventh and twelfth centuries (Best and O'Brien 1967, 1298) with their ancestor Áed mac Ainmerech (killed in 598). Ua Domnaill supremacy after the reign of Éicnechán (1201–8) was firmly established by his son Domnall Mór, king of Tír Conaill and Fir Manach from 1201 to 1208.

Cathbarr's own name may have had special significance. An early hymn to Colum Cille ascribed to Adomnán and later referred to by Maghnus Ó Domhnaill is called a *cathbarr,* or helmet, in two manuscripts that derive from the lost twelfth-century Book of Glendalough (Carney 1964, xiii). The twelfth-century saga of the Death of Muirchertach Mac Erca (Nic Dhonnchadha 1964, 8) refers to the *Cathach*, in the hands of the Cenél Conaill, as one of the three battle-standards (*meirge*) of the Uí Néill, the others being the Bell of St Patrick's Testament (enshrined by Domnall Ua Lochlainn in the 1090s) and the medieval shrine known as the *Mísach* of St Cairnech of Dulane near Kells.

The Mac Robhartaigh[7] family was probably given lands at the Columban church of Drumhome (Ballymagrorty) near Ballyshannon in the thirteenth century by the Uí Dhomhnaill when that family moved to nearby Assaroe to plant the former Ua Canannáin and Ua Mael Doraid lands. It can be suggested that the *Cathach* was at Drumhome as early as the middle of the thirteenth century on the basis of a poem contained in the Book of Fenagh (Hennessy and Kelly 1875,166–171) that mentions Drumhome and the *Cathach* manuscript, attributing the writing of it to Colum Cille. It appears that the *Cathach* was kept in a crypt under a late church in the townland of Ballymagrorty Scotch that was demolished in the nineteenth century, the ancient Ráth Cunga (Racoon) (Ó Cochláin 1968, 161), a Patrician foundation where Assicus of Elphin and Rathlin O'Birne was buried *c.* 500.

What may be an oblique reference to the *Cathach* is found in a poem written about 1230 by Giolla Brighde mac Con Midhe (Williams 1980, 18) in which there is mention of the *lúireach* (breastplate) of Colum Cille; described as the words of Colum Cille in battle (*briathra Colaim Chille i gcath*), this may echo the early hymn to Colum Cille, ascribed to Adomnán, which is called a *cathbarr* or helmet. The later poem was written in praise of

---

[7] Mac Robhartaigh is the modern Irish spelling of mac Robartaig; the name is anglicised, in variant spellings, as Roarty, McRoarty, McGroarty, Magroarty.

Domhnall Mór Ó Domhnaill, king of Tír Conaill and Fir Manach from 1208 to 1241. His line continued through his son Domhnall Óg (1258–61), grandson Aodh (1281–1333), great-grandson Seán (1362–80) and great-great-grandson Toirdealbhach an Fhíona (1380–1422). The line is further traced through Toirdealbhach an Fhiona's son Niall Garbh (1422–39). Of these figures, Toirdealbhach an Fhíona, who appointed the Ó Cléirigh family as historians to the Ó Domhnaill family, had the kind of prominence that makes him a likely candidate to have refurbished the *Cathach* with a new top plate that resembles fourteenth-century work on the shrine known as the *Domhnach Airgid* (Armstrong and Lawlor 1918).

The *Cathach* was captured and its *maor* (keeper) Mac Robhartaigh slain at the battle of Bealach Buidhe near Boyle in 1497, when the Ó Domhnaill family were defeated by MacDermot of Moylurg. It was brought to the battle of Fearsad Mór (near Letterkenny) fought between O'Neill and O'Donnell in 1567, when its custodian, another Mac Robhartaigh, was slain (AFM). Colgan (1647, 495) wrote that in his time the *Cathach* was kept at Ballymagrorty in the parish of Drumhome. It was carried away from Tír Conaill by Colonel Daniel O'Donel of Ramelton, who followed King James II to France after the Battle of the Boyne in 1690. O'Donel had the *cumhdach* refurbished and inscribed on the Continent in 1723; he also engraved the O'Donel arms on a semi-circular projection midway along the front of the base (as described by Armstrong in Lawlor 1916, 395–6). The coat of arms is a version similar to that granted to O'Donel in a certificate of arms by the Athlone Pursuivant at the Jacobite court at St Germain-en-Laye, James Terry, in 1709 (Hayes 1949, 296–7). O'Donel died on 7 July 1735, leaving a widow and a fourteen-year-old daughter.

George Petrie (OSL, 216) records that before his death Daniel O'Donel deposited the *Cathach* in a monastery, which can plausibly be identified as the convent of the Irish Benedictine nuns at Ypres in Flanders (modern Belgium) (Herity 2000, 462). This convent had close connections with the court of James III: a Mr O'Donnell was appointed confessor there in 1701 by the Dowager Queen Mary (Historical Manuscripts Commission 1902, 161). It can be assumed that some doubts as to who the legitimate heir to the title 'The O'Donnell' might be and who would therefore be entitled to the keepership of the *Cathach* led

O'Donel to take the unusual step of depositing the manuscript there; he stipulated in writing that it should be given up to the chief of the clan when applied for (OSL, 216).

It appears that the reliquary was seen at the 'monastery' by Father Prendergast, Parish Priest and titular Augustinian Abbot of Cong from 1795, who, it has been implied, was a seminarian at nearby St Omer (Wilde 1867, 174n.), probably in the 1760s. He informed Sir Neal O'Donel of Newport, County Mayo, who had bought the former abbey lands at Cong in 1780 (Ó Cochláin 1968, 171). Sir Neal applied for the *Cathach* as chief of the family but was required to provide a certificate attested by Sir William Betham, Deputy Ulster King of Arms, to support his claim; the *Cathach* was handed over in 1813 to his brother Connel O'Donel, who was then on the continent (OSL, 216).

Betham (1826, 109–10) described in his *Irish antiquarian researches* how he examined the metal shrine with the ready permission of 'its present possessor, Connel O'Donell, Esq.'. Disregarding 'injunctions and threats of ignorance, which for more than a century had hermetically sealed it up, under an idea that it contained the bones of St. Columkill himself…the box was opened and examined in the presence of Sir Capel Molyneux, Mr O'Donell, and myself, without any extraordinary, or supernatural occurrence…'. Inside he found the manuscript, covered on one side with 'a thin piece of board covered with red leather, very like that with which eastern MSS. are bound'. As folio 58v, the last surviving page of the manuscript, bears traces of abrasion, probably from contact with the metal of the shrine, it seems likely that the cover of red leather on board had lain at the front of the surviving membranes.

The following scenario can be proposed to reconcile various accounts of the return of the *Cathach* to Ireland—Betham's (1826, 20–21, 109–10, 189), Petrie's (OSL, 216), O'Donovan's (AFM, 2400) and O'Curry's (1861, 331). Continual war between 1802 and 1813 made access to Flanders difficult. Sir Capel Molyneux, son-in-law of Sir Neal O'Donel, and his wife, Margaret, had sought out the *Cathach* at a monastery in Flanders during the short-lived peace that followed the Treaty of Amiens in 1802. As Petrie has recorded, proof was required of the right of the O'Donels of Newport to keepership of the relic before it would be released. In 1805 William Betham came to Dublin and later became Deputy Ulster King of Arms; he was knighted in

1812. The certificate 'To All and Singular' at the end of an O'Donnell genealogy, now in the Royal Irish Academy and attested by Betham on 30 September 1813, is probably the one mentioned by Petrie as the authority that Connel O'Donel required to claim and acquire the *Cathach* from the monastery in Flanders late in that year. A copy of this genealogy and its proofs in MS G.O. 169 of the Genealogical Office, Dublin, is also dated 30 September 1813. It would appear that the shrine came to Ireland only after this genealogy was made. The opening of the shrine and the discovery of the psalter, which Betham describes as having taken place in his study in Blackrock, County Dublin, in the presence of Mr Connel O'Donel and Sir Capel Molyneux, can be dated to 1813 by the Bill of Complaint filed against Betham for opening the shrine by Dame Mary O'Donel on 30 April 1814; these events apparently took place in the last months of 1813. Betham first tested his hypothesis that the shrine contained a manuscript by passing a 'slender wire' through a small opening, with which he rubbed the edges of the vellum leaves (Lawlor 1916, 244 nn 2, 3). This scenario requires that the drawings of the top and base of the shrine that appear in both of Betham's manuscript genealogies were probably added later.

The initials of the *Cathach*

Each of the surviving psalms in the *Cathach* has a rubric or heading of up to three lines written in orange minium in a space left for it by the scribe; sometimes the words are spread out to fill the space, sometimes the writing is closely crowded, occasionally it overruns the space allotted (Lawlor 1916, 252). Beneath the heading, the text of the psalm begins with an ornamented initial followed by up to three further ornamented letters (Fig. 4). Unlike those in classical manuscripts, these initials are placed within the block of psalm text, some extending as many as six lines down, some extending upwards into the text of the heading. The initials also assume an intimate relationship with the text through a series of diminishing intermediate letters. The fact that many of the 150 psalms begin with one of the same small group of letters presented a formidable challenge to the inventiveness of the Irish scribe, who wished each ornamented initial to be an original and unique creation. As Pächt (1986, 51) has observed, letters are symbols that must be understood clearly, and there is

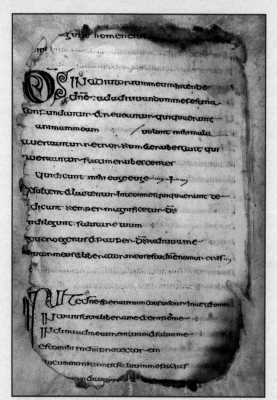

Fig. 4—Fol. 30v of the *Cathach*, showing rubrics and decorated initials of Psalms 69 and 70.

therefore a limit beyond which ornamentation should not be carried.

The great majority of these initials are based on the uncial, or majuscule, forms of the letters, and the artist wishing to devise ornamental versions was both limited and liberated by their forms. Sixty-five initials have survived, intact or fragmentary (see Figs 5–10 for a selection of the initials). Traces of a dotted outline in minium, which in most cases has retained its orange colour but in a few has turned brown, can now be discerned on up to 47 of these, most of them well-preserved examples. Painting in the body of the letter in a white colour tinged with pink is more difficult to discern with certainty but seems to occur in 35 initials, including two instances where a light red, possibly minium, is used. There is more room for doubt in the early folios of the

Fol. 26r

Fol. 43v

Fol. 35r

Fol. 30v

Fig. 5—Initial *I* (fols 26r, 43v); initial *N* (fol. 35r); *N* not in initial position (fols 30v, 43v). On fol. 43v *INCL*: *I* and *N* are both surrounded by dotting. On fol. 30v *IN te dñe*: *I* and *N* are surrounded by dotting; cross-member of *N* shows clear traces of orange.

manuscript, up to about fol. 28v; it may be that the blotting-paper used by Betham (1826, 111) to separate the folios after the discover of the manuscript has obscured a greater proportion of the features of these early folios. The limited technical resources available to Lawlor (1916, 252) led him to count only 20 initials with traces of colour in the body of the letter and 42 outlined with orange dots. Where the half-uncial letter forms are used, the motivation may have been a desire for diversity; alternatively, this form may have presented the artist with a more suitable model for ornamentation, as in the case of the letter *B*. It appears that an edged quill of the type used for writing the book-hand of the text was also used for the thick down-strokes; here too it was held at a fairly flat angle to the horizontal, as is evidenced in the alignment of the thin oblique strokes of the initial *O* of fol. 14v. Whereas such initials as those on fols 4r and 13r seem to have been formed with a single downstroke, many other verticals were doubled to achieve the desired thickness; this was also achieved by filling between two outer lines, as in the lower left-hand member of the initial *U* on fol. 35v.

Those initials that are based on upright columns necessarily depart little from the classic form of the letter: they include the five examples of initial *I* (fols 4r, 11v, 26r, 30v, 43v), the two of initial *N* (fols 6r, 35r) and the six of initial *Q* (fols 11r, 18r, 32v, 40r, 42v, 48r). Initial *I* is tall, up to five line spaces in height; it is composed of two verticals made with the quill, between which an open space is left for painting; it narrows from top to bottom and has a slight freehand curve; the top is finished with a spiral-ended yoke, Duval's *accolade* (Duval 1977, 284), the lower end with a thin tail tending left. The treatment is freehand, the shape influenced by the wedge-shaped serif found on smaller versions of the letter, and with curvilinear embellishments at the ends.

In the two examples of initial *N* a longer left-hand vertical column five line spaces in height is treated in the same manner as initial *I* but with elaborations of the lower end based on Irish La Tène motifs.[8] The right-hand vertical column is shorter, with spiral elaborations at the upper end; in each of the two initial *N*s

---

[8] The La Tène flourished in central Europe in the late Iron Age and came to pre-Christian Ireland *c*. 300 BC. Its distinctive curvilinear style was evident in the stone and metal work, weaponry and decorative art of this period and also carried on into the early Christian period in Ireland.

Fol. 42r

Fol. 11r

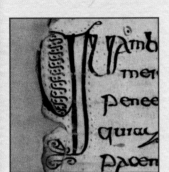

Fol. 32v

Fol. 40r

Fol. 52v

Fig. 6—Half-uncial *D* (fol. 42r); initial *Q* (fols 11r, 32v, 40r); initial *D* with animal head (fol. 52v). On fol. 42r *D* and *S* are both surrounded by faint dotting. On fol. 11r see lower left of spiral in *Q* where doubled pen line can be seen in magnification. On fol. 32v each of the first four letters (*QUAM*) is surrounded by dotting. On fol. 40r initial *Q* is surrounded by faint dotting; a zoomorphic impression is created by the eye-dot in the embellishment at the lower end. On fol. 52v initial *D* is surrounded by dots. Note the *trompe l'oeil* effect created by the neck of the beast.

it is joined to the taller left-hand column by a curved, eyed fish-like element with spiral tail. The uncial *N* of *Inclina* (fol. 43v) is treated similarly: its S-curved, fish-like element joins the base of the shorter right-hand column to the head of the longer left-hand one and has a collar as well as an eye. The columns in the *N* of *In te dñe* (fol. 30v) are joined in the same manner with an S-curved fish, eyed and collared, partly painted in orange. These versions of *N* are forerunners of the more elaborate version of Codex Ambr. S 45 sup., p. 2 (Henry 1950, fig. 1; Henderson 1987, 25–8) and Durham MS A.II.10, both dated to the early seventh century, where this fish has developed into an intertwined double-headed beast (Henry 1965, pl. 61). As Henry put it:

> The extreme importance of the
> Cathach…comes from the fact that it allows
> us to grasp what the decoration of manuscripts
> was before the contacts with the Continent had
> become closer, and much before the
> development of the Northumbrian scriptoria.
> (Henry 1965, 61)

The upright column of each of the five substantially intact *Q*s (fols 11r, 32v, 40r, 42v, 48r) is similar to the uprights of *I* and *N*. In one case (fol. 48r) it has a solid body and zoomorphic counter-curve to the spiral tail; the upper end of the column has a half-yoke embellishment (Duval's *pseudo-accolade*) similar to a flourish found on some of the initials of the sixth-century Laurentian manuscript of Orosius, Plutarch 65 (Nordenfalk 1947, 153–5, figs. 10, 11, 13). In some cases the ovoid element, formed by a pair of curved lines made with a broad quill, has a narrow vertical open space intended to be painted. Each has a filler motif in the open field within the oval, either a dotted chevron—a v-shaped ornamentation (fols 11r, 42v)—or a dotted chain (fols 32v, 40r, 48r) like that forming the frame of the cross-ornamented page of the Codex Usserianus Primus (Trinity College, Dublin) (Henry 1965, pl. 58), a manuscript assigned by Lowe (CLA[2], 42) to the beginning of the seventh century. The two letters *D* that follow the half-uncial form (fols 27r, 42r) are made in similar fashion to the *Q*s but with a plainer treatment of the base of the column. One (fol. 27r) has a dotted chain filler, the other a chevron.

Fol. 15v

Fol. 36v

Fol. 52r

Fol. 22r

Fol. 21v

Fig. 7—Initial *A* (fols 15v, 36v) together with metalwork technique (fol. 52r); *C* (fol. 52r), *E* (fol. 22r) and *S* (fol. 21v). On fol. 15v the uprights of the letter *A* are filled with paint; the first two letters are dotted. On fol. 36v a very elaborate initial *A* is constructed of zoomorphic elements including a beast partially shown at the bottom left. On fol. 52r initial *C* has an upper element reminiscent of metalwork. The outlines of this bold initial are dotted. On fol. 22r the bold shape of the initial *C* is adapted to form an *E* by the addition of a fish, swimming. On fol. 21v initial *S* and many of the letters that follow it are decorated with dotting.

Five *C*s (fols 34v, 51r, 52r, 56v, 58r) and six *E*s (fols 13r, 22r, 23v, 25r, 27r, 41r) survive as decorative initials. Each shaft is based on a vertical line set on the right within a thicker curved crescent, leaving a narrow space between; these lines cross over at the top to form the downturn at the top right of the letter, embellished with a spiral-ended yoked flourish, biased towards the right. At the base they taper to a small spiral in all cases except one (fol. 51r), where the yoke of the upper end of the *C* is repeated in miniature at the lower end. The *E*s have an extra member in the form of a tiny fish as the middle arm of the letter, two of which (fols 22r, 23v) have an eye-circle. The only initial *F* (fol. 44r) is of a similar form, with an upper curved member springing to the right from the top right-hand corner of a paired-line column and terminating in an asymmetrical yoke. The lower horizontal member of this *F* is also a fish-like curve.

The fragmentary *T* of fol. 25v follows the half-uncial form and ends in a small, tight spiral. It is constructed of two pairs of curved lines, each pair bounding an open space. The space is filled by a row of dots, as in La Tène metalwork. The only surviving initial *O* (fol. 14v) is of simple construction, drawn with pairs of lines bounding an open space at the upper right and lower left. The *m* of the word *Omnes* and the first four letters of the first word on the next line, *iubilate*, fill its inner space, suggesting that the initial *O* was made first in this case. Another *o* (fol. 34v), not in initial position and drawn with a thick line, is filled with a dotted chain motif down its centre.

The remaining initials, *D, B, U, S, M* and *A*, lend themselves to a curvilinear mode more in keeping with La Tène forms and style. In eighteen uncial initial *D*s (fols 7v, 8v, 12r, 14r, 18v, 19r, 23r, 24v, 30v, 39v, 41v, 44v, 47r, 49r, 49v, 51v, 52v, 53v) the basic circle or oval is usually two-and-a-half line spaces in depth, with the curved triangular ascender extending as much as two line spaces above and to the left. Double lines with open spaces within form both vertical sides of the circular element; where the triangular ascender is preserved it often has a curved yoke flourish at the end. In one case (fol. 19r) the ascender, itself a pelta, or representation of a whale's tail, contains a second, tiny, painted pelta; in another (fol. 44v) it merges into what appears to be a spiral-ended cross form. In all cases there is an attempt to fill the open circular space: eight *D*s (fols 7v, 14r, 19r, 23r, 24v, 41v, 44v, 51v) and a possible ninth (fol. 47r) have dotted chain motifs;

Fol. 43r

Fol. 55v

Fol. 35v

Fol. 12r

Fol. 19r

Fig. 8—Initial *B* (fols 43r, 55v); initial *U* (fol. 35v); uncial *D* (fols 12r, 19r). On fol. 43r, traces of dotting are visible around the first letters of *BENEDIXISTI*. On fol. 55v, dots outline the *B*, which has two trumpet-curves meeting at a lentoid, bottom left. On fol. 35v there are traces of paint in the right-hand upright, which ends in a double inturned spiral design at the upper end; the orange dotting is well marked. On fol. 12r the letter *D* is built on the fulcrum of a pelta. On fol. 19r the use of paint to fill major spaces in the *D* and to highlight details like the pelta (top left) and the triangles at the ends of the letter *S* is well demonstrated. The faintest traces of dotting remain around the outer edge of the initial.

three (fols 8v, 39v, 52v) have spirals—one (fol. 52v) incorporates part of a stylised animal head, the other two end in La Tène trumpet counter-curves; three further examples (fols 18v, 30v, 49v) have simple La Tène trumpets; two (fols 12r, 53v) have peltas. The most elaborate example (fol. 19r) has a pair of trumpets meeting at a lentoid, or lens-shaped element, in the right-hand side of the circle and a similar angled expansion in the pair of lines opposite, echoing a feature of the treatment of initials *B* and *U* described below.

Each of the five decorated initial *B*s (fols 3r, 43r, 48v, 54v, 55v) consists of a lower circular element, drawn with paired lines on the upper right and lower left, with a wide vertical trumpet-shaped ascender; in three cases (fols 43r, 48v, 55v) the ascender is elaborated by a yoke rising above it to the left or right. Four (fol. 43r, 48v, 54v, 55v) were designed with a distinctive sharp angle towards the lower left-hand side, in one case (fol. 55v) marked by a lentoid. While this form can be seen as influenced by the half-uncial letter, which has a straight vertical left-hand member like the modern lower-case letter *b*, the concept underlying the structure is equally plausibly a design formed of three La Tène elements: a pair of trumpets meeting in the lower left-hand corner, e.g. at the lentoid of fol. 55v, and a spiral-ended crescent closing the oval element of the letter at the top right. In three cases the space in the circular element is filled with decoration: a dotted chain (fol. 54v), a further trumpet-like motif, counter-curved and partially surviving (fol. 3r), and a triskele (fol. 43r).

The three *U*s (fols 33v, 35v, 50v) are based on a vertical columnar member on the right and a curvilinear member on the left. In two cases (fols 33v and 50v) the upper terminals of each column have a spiral-ended yoke-like flourish that is biased to the right; the third has a symmetrical pair of inturned spirals. Each column also has a yoked embellishment at the lower end. The bottom left side of one example (fol. 35v), and probably of a second (fol. 50v), is angled and, like the letter *B*, trumpet-based in concept.

S is represented twice as a decorative initial (fols 21v, 28v) and elsewhere as a decorative letter not in initial position. In each case it appears that the uncial form was used, based on a pair of spirals each with a triangular projection ending in a long flourish, like versions of *S* in the Ambrosian Codex S 45 sup. (Henry 1950,

Fol. 17v

Fol. 20v

Fol. 53r

Fig. 9—Initial *M* (fols 17v, 20v, 53r). In the *M* on fol. 17v the central column and the curved upright element on the right are painted; orange dotting outlines the letter; the circles are compass-drawn— the central perforation left by the dividers shows on fol. 17r. The *M* on fol. 20v also appears to be compass-drawn; a scratched line made by the dividers shows between the line of dots and the inner edge of the curved line, bottom right. On fol. 53r, the initial *M* stands on three pairs of apposed spirals and is outlined with orange dotting; a number of curved quill-strokes can be seen in the far right-hand upright element.

fig. 10; see further discussion of this manuscript on pp 29 and 37 below). The upper terminal of the fragmentary example of *S* on fol. 28v is filled with traces of what can be reconstructed as a cross with expanded terminals (see Fig. 11a below). The triangular appendage above is conceived as two trumpets meeting at a lentoid that is filled with three dots in line.

There are five surviving examples of *M* in initial position (fols 17v, 20v, 21r, 45r, 53r). In three monumental constructions of the letter (fols 17v, 20v, 21r), and possibly in a fourth fragmentary *M* of the same type (fol. 45r), the uncial form is elaborated in the curvilinear idiom of Irish La Tène. A central column with concave sides supports on either side circular forms based on compass-drawn circles with pairs of vertically-set curved lines enclosing a narrow painted space. Within the circles of fol. 21r a pair of spirals is formed, the counter-curve emerging from each spiral swelling to a lentoid between two trumpet curves. The design of the *M* of fol. 20v is similar, while the *M* on fol. 17v has a simpler design in which the outer elements curve around into the centre of each circle to meet the convex mouth of a simple trumpet. The example on fol. 53r, the half-uncial initial *M* of Psalm 100, is a brilliantly simple version of the letter with zoomorphic overtones, a playful three-footed creation shod with symmetric double spirals and with an S-curved tail.

Two initial *A*s (fols 15v, 36v), each based on the uncial form, are elaborate structures. Both are formed of two major fish-like curved elements, each enclosing an open space between curved lines, the longer, lower, vertical element joining the upper, diagonal one about half-way along its underside. These elements are joined by a third, tiny, fish-like curve that closes the *A* near the base of the diagonal fish above. Each *A* is bounded by thick lines: in the less elaborate one (fol. 15v) each main element consists of a single pair of lines with painting between, the lower end of each ending in a flourish; the more elaborate *A* (fol. 36v) has double paired lines defining the two major elements, with thicker lines on the inside of the upper element, which also has an eye-circle and a collar. An open-mouthed 'beast' can be reconstructed, curling round from the lowermost extremity of the letter.

Two further fragmentary crosses associated with initial letters have been detected in the *Cathach* since Lawlor's study. Traces of the upper limb and right arm of the first are discernible on fol. 28v in the surviving upper fragment of the initial letter *S* of *Salvum* in

Fol. 6r

Fol. 48r

Fol. 50v

Fig. 10—Equal-armed crosses standing on uprights in and on the initials on fols 6r, 48r and 50v.

Psalm 68 (Fig. 11a), where two characteristic pointed curves can be viewed as part of a tiny cross that is very similar to those depicted on fols 48r and 50v. The second cross (Fig. 11b), noted by Roth (1979, 68), is more fully preserved: it forms an extension of the end of the initial *D* of *Domine Deus* in Psalm 87 (fol. 44v). It has an expanded arm like those of the other crosses but appears to have been surmounted at the upper end of the shaft by a pair of inturned spirals (like those of the initial *U* on fol. 35v). These spirals are now separated from the head by a tear in the

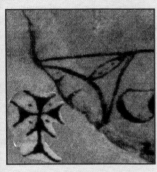

Fol. 28v

Fol. 44v

Fig. 11—Partially-defined crosses in initials: fol. 28v—probable remains of cross with expanded terminals in initial *S* of *Salvum*, with cross from fol. 50v inset for comparison; fol. 44v—equal-armed cross with inturned spiral scrolls at head and probably at the foot shown with tentative reconstruction in white.

parchment; a curve, lower right, suggests that there was originally a pair of similar spirals at the lower end of the shaft. Small dots in the two remaining cantons probably belong to a set of four, as in fol. 50v.

The main inspiration in the design of many of the initials is Irish La Tène, freehand and lively, occasionally playful. Lentoid and lobeate swellings, the triple-dot motif, trumpet ends, curve and counter-curve, peltae and spiral ends (simple or at the ends of a yoked motif) and Duval's *accolade* are almost universal. The theory that Celtic metalwork influenced the design of the initials is strongly supported by the occurrence of background hachuring or dotting in fols 25v, 30v, 40r, 48r and 52r as well as the triple-dot motifs of fols 7v, 14v, 23v, 33v and the initial *D* of fol. 52v. These triangular triple-dot arrangements in orange repeat a motif found in the free spaces of the design of a pagan Celtic scabbard-plate from the river Bann (Raftery 1983, 103–4) and are also found in the Bobbio manuscripts and later manuscripts like the books of Durrow, Lindisfarne and Kells.

The use of compasses, well known in the pre-Christian metalwork tradition, is evidenced in the design of two initial *M*s, fols 17v and 21r (Fig. 12). The centre points of the two circles in the *M* of fol. 21r are marked by dots immediately above the spiral in each (Fig. 12b). On the verso of the folio each of these dots is matched by a smaller one. Circles described on these as centres extend from the edges of the central pillar to the inner of the two lines marking the upright crescents of the *M*. This observation has been confirmed by Mr Anthony Cains (pers. comm.), Head of Conservation at the Library, Trinity College, Dublin, who has discerned under magnification perforations marked by these dots and scratched lines under the ink at points along the circumference of both circles. These marks can be explained by the use of a pair of dividers, an item of equipment that would have been commonplace in a scriptorium and that was used for the pricking and ruling of each gathering of this manuscript. The centre points of the similar, though fragmentary, initial *M* on fol. 17v (Fig. 12a) are visible on the verso of the page and match the spot where the curved line meets the wedge of the pelta in each circle. A circle described on the point of the intact right-hand circle runs from the edge of the central pillar to the outer line of the upright crescent on the right. It appears that both *M*s were designed on symmetrical pairs of compass-drawn circles that were so faintly marked that they can now be barely discerned. On fol. 20v an arc of a circle etched immediately to the right of the line of dots inside the inner right-hand curved line suggests the use of dividers in the laying-out of this *M* too. The *Cathach* thus looks back towards a design technique well known in Irish La Tène metalwork and forward to a later manuscript tradition in which designs based on the use of compasses continue the earlier traditions (Henry 1965, 206–24).

A separate, restricted set of exotic influences comes from early Christian art: manuscript conventions are represented in the forms of the initials themselves, in the Coptic dotting surrounding them and in chain and chevron filler patterns. The single spiral extension at the base of the right-hand column of the initial *U* of fol. 35v may derive from symmetrical paired spiral extensions like those at the ends of the arms of the Coptic ankh

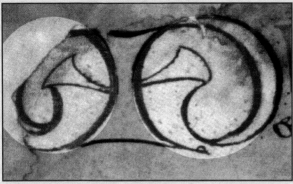

Fol. 17v

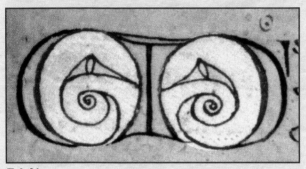

Fol. 21r

Fig. 12—Compass-drawn designs for initial *M* on fols 17v and 21r. The basic compass-drawn circles are shown in a lighter shade in each case.

of the Glazier Codex of *c*. AD 400 (Bober 1967, fig. 1). One of the five crosses that intrude into the design of a number of initials has paired symmetric spirals at least at the upper end of the shaft (fol. 44v); the others are of a simpler type with flaring terminals. A design element also greatly favoured by the scribe is a simple, fluid fish motif, often eyed, occasionally with a collar, the early Christian ιχθύς, which is rendered in a more developed form in the Bobbio manuscripts Ambrosian I 61 sup. and S 45 sup. This last manuscript, Atalanus's, also has the triple-dot motif at the foot of the column of the initial *P* and on the body of the 'fish' (Henry 1950, fig. 20*b*, *c*). In the *Cathach* this fish is frequently used as the cross-member of the letters *E, F* and *N* and is the basic design element in the two examples of initial *A*. The zoomorphic eye in the left-hand crescent of the *D* on fol. 51v also suggests a fish of this family. In just a few cases, fols 48r and 52v, the 'fish' is given a characteristic open beast-mouth. Is it possible to interpret these as dolphins?

These two sources, pagan Celtic and early Christian, contribute to the design of two contrasting sets of letters, one broadly columnar, the other broadly curvilinear. The *N*, its bold uprights joined by a fish cross-member, is typical of the first group, the compass-based *M*, with its trumpet, spiral and triskele fillers, of the second. Almost every initial is informed by a Celtic style, freehand, tending to the curvilinear, with asymmetric curved elaborations. The Christian fish, often simplified, is incorporated in a fluid Celtic rhythm, a feature most clearly visible in the design of both initial *A*s. In a *trompe l'oeil* detail typical of Irish Celtic art, the neck of the collared fish-beast in the initial *D* of *DÑS* on fol. 52v disappears into the void as the eye follows it outwards. Of all the manuscripts of early date from Ireland or Irish centres on the Continent, the *Cathach* shows in its initials the greatest influence of the Celtic style.

Comparanda in stone and other media for crosses in the *Cathach*

A distinctive addition to three of the decorative initials of the *Cathach* is a tiny cross with wide expanded terminals ending in points, each standing on a stem with a greatly expanded foot. One stands within the *N* of *Noli*, the first word of Psalm 36 (fol. 6r), a second stands behind the head of a fishy beast forming part of the initial *Q* of *Qui habitat*, Psalm 90 (fol. 48r), a third, with dots in each of the four cantons, sits inside the *U* of *Uenite* at the beginning of Psalm 93 (fol. 50v). A parallel for the combination of cross and dolphin on fol. 48r can be found in the Coptic world (at Armant, Egypt), in a Latin cross with expanded ends shown behind the head of a fish depicted with mouth widely splayed; this stone panel (Fig. 13) is dated to the fifth or sixth century (Badawy 1978, 186, fig. 3.140). The discovery of two further crosses (fols 28v, 44v) is noted above (see Fig. 11), the second of these being a more elaborate form apparently with inturned spirals.

Very similar crosses with expanded terminals ornament the paired terminals of four penannular brooches in the National

Fig. 13—Latin cross and Coptic fish from Armant, Egypt (Musée du Louvre, Paris). (© Photo RMN—B. Hatala)

Museum of Ireland (Fig. 14a–d). One of these is from County Westmeath (Fig. 14a), the other three are from unknown locations in Ireland (Haseloff 1990, 158). Two of those found at unknown locations are depicted standing on stems like those in the *Cathach* crosses (Fig. 14b, d). Duignan (1973) has reported a pair of broadly similar crosses pattée (i.e. with expanded terminals) a little over 3mm wide at either end of an *S*-scroll and within a curved rectangular band, presumably originally enamelled, on a bronze hand-pin from Treanmacmurtagh Bog in County Sligo (Fig. 14e), which she assigns to her Class IIIb. A similar stamped design on an imported pottery dish from the monastery of Tintagel in Cornwall is discussed below (p. 36).

A latchet-fastener from Ireland noted by Wilde (1861, 566–7, W.491) and dated to the fifth or sixth century has a six-petalled marigold at the centre of its disk, and the designs between the petals have the same cusped expansion at the outer ends and the same narrowing profile as the limbs of the crosses pattée on the terminals of the pennannular brooches drawn by Haseloff; the whole design of the centre of the disk is surrounded by a single incised line arranged in swags with triple-dot motifs at the points. Cross and marigold are closely related designs in early Christian

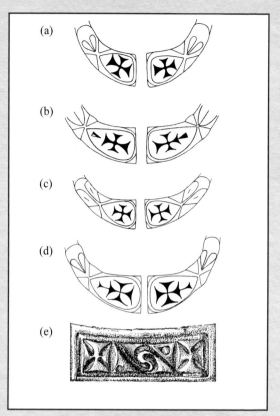

Fig. 14—Cross-ornamented terminals of penannular brooches: (a) County Westmeath; (b), (c), (d) Ireland (after Haseloff 1990); (e) detail of hand-pin from Treanmacmurtagh Bog, Sligo (after Duignan 1973).

Ireland, the one often appearing as the obverse of the other, as on a great prehistoric standing stone at Killeen in County Mayo (Herity 1995b, 235, pl. 3) and at the centre of the carpet page (fol. 85v) of the Book of Durrow.

In stone there are excellent comparanda: on a broken slab from the fifth-century foundation of St Mochaoi of Nendrum in Strangford Lough, County Down (Fig. 15a); on a boulder, part of a prehistoric burial monument at Knockane on the Dingle peninsula in County Kerry (Herity 1995b, 240–1, pl. 5.3) (Fig. 15b); and within a penannular cartouche with spiral ends on a boulder at the ecclesiastical site of Kilvickadownig at the west end of the same peninsula (Cuppage *et al.* 1986, 327, fig. 196) (Fig. 15c), where the cross stands on a stem like those of the *Cathach*. Another closely comparable cross on stem within a circular cartouche is carved on a boulder in the early ecclesiastical site at Maumanorig on the same peninsula (Cuppage *et al.* 1986, 332–3, fig. 201a) (Fig. 15d); here an ogham inscription belonging to the later post-syncope series and engraved in an unusual fashion on a curved stem-line may have been added later than the elaborate cross—Macalister (1945, 186–8) has read the inscription as *ANM COLMAN AILITHIR* ('the name of Colman the pilgrim').

A similar tiny crosslet with characteristic expanded ends is deeply engraved within a circle on a small water-worn boulder, apparently a prayer-stone or so-called 'cursing-stone', in the oratory of Senach's island foundation of Illauntannig, one of the Maharees group of islands, opposite Kilshannig, off the north coast of the Dingle peninsula (Fig. 16). A simple carving with similar expanded ends existed at Conwal in Donegal (Lacy *et al.* 1983, 258, fig. 136, pl. 36). Henry (1951, 67, 69, fig. 2) has compared the Latin cross with expanded terminals standing on a short stem depicted on her Pillar 12 on top of the Bailey Mór on

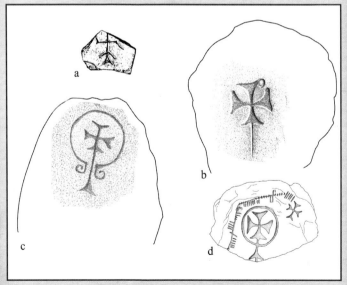

Fig. 15—Cross-engraved slabs: (a) Nendrum, (b) Knockane, (c) Kilvickadownig, (d) Maumanorig (after Cuppage *et al.* 1986).

the island of Inishkea North, off the Mullet peninsula in Mayo, with the cross-on-stem depicted on fol. 48r (Psalm 90) of the *Cathach*. A similar equal-armed cross with widely expanded terminals on the arms and shaft stands in relief on a pillar and slight base on the architrave of the doorway of the church at Clonamery in County Kilkenny. This has been compared to Armenian and Georgian crosses of the fifth to seventh centuries (Richardson 1987, 134–5).

This distinctive form of the cross was apparently widespread in Ireland, being found in counties Kerry, Westmeath, Mayo, Sligo, Donegal and Down, and is associated with early monastic foundations like Nendrum. It was particularly well known in the non-Patrician south-west (Herity 1995b, 252). Its occurrence on penannular brooches (an early form derived from Roman brooches), in a cognate form on a latchet, on a hand-pin and carved on stone slabs and pillars at ecclesiastical sites associated with early saints of the fifth and sixth centuries suggests that the models for these crosses could have been introduced substantially before 600 and may well have been in fashion

Fig. 16—Illauntannig prayer-stone with engraved cross.

throughout the sixth century, in the second half of which Colum Cille flourished. The dominance of Irish La Tène motifs and style in the ornamentation of the initials of the *Cathach* compared with the scarcity of elements introduced from the Christian world outside Ireland supports this assessment.

An equal-armed cross on a stem engraved on a stone slab located near St Columba's Church on Inishkea North (Fig. 17), Henry's Slab 5 (Henry 1945, 145, Pl. XXVIII, bottom right), has decorative terminals resembling those found on some of the *Cathach* initials. Here the solid ends of the arms, shaft and foot of the stand are decorated by adding a wide yoke terminating in a tiny spiral at either end, not unlike Duval's *accolade*, as found on the *E* of *Eripe* on fol. 22r (Psalm 58) and the *N* of *Notus* on fol. 35r (Psalm 75). A Latin cross standing on a pedestal between two globes on a Byzantine medallion dated to the first half of the fifth century, now in the Walters Art Gallery in Baltimore (Haseloff

Fig. 17—Engraved cross on stone pillar on Inishkea North (Henry 1945, pl. XXVIII, bottom right).

1990, 16, fig. 2), and one depicted between apposed birds in the north Italian Gospel-Book of Valerianus, now in Munich (Nordenfalk 1947, fig. 6), have similar terminals at the head and the ends of the arms. The footed *Crux Ansata* of the Coptic Glazier Codex, *c.* AD 400, in which coloured ribbon interlace appears as an integral element of illumination, also has similar spiral terminals, which are recognised by Bober (1967, 40–42, fig. 1) as typical of the period and characteristic of decorative pen-work in early manuscripts of Egyptian origin. This yoke with spiral ends is seen in developed form on the upper end of the cross-slab erected on Station 10 at Caher Island, a little to the south of the Inishkea islands (Herity 1995a, 120, fig. 30). While the Inishkea slab could be interpreted as influenced by pagan Celtic yoked designs, it is more likely, given the fact that it is footed, that the whole design, including the yokes, is derived from a cross model very like that depicted on the Baltimore medallion, in the Glazier Codex and in the Gospel-Book of Valerianus.

There is archaeological evidence of not inconsiderable trade in materials imported directly from the north-east Mediterranean to Ireland; travellers and material culture from there probably came to Ireland with the currents generated by this trade at a date relatively early in our Christian period. Wine and oil amphorae of Type Bii from Cilicia and from Antioch in ancient Syria—which, along with Jerusalem and Alexandria, was one of the three Patriarchates of the earliest Christian Church in the east Mediterranean—and Phocaean tableware of Type Ai dated between 475 and 550 from the adjacent area of modern Turkey have been found together at ecclesiastical sites and as a new feature at long-established royal and trading centres in south-west Britain and Ireland (Thomas 1959; 1981; Fulford 1989). Ralegh Radford (1956, pl. VI, A, bottom right) records crosses, one with expanded terminals like those of the *Cathach*, stamped on the inner surface of pottery dishes of Class Ai from the early monastery at Tintagel in Cornwall. These imported dishes may have had their place in Christian ritual as patens used in the Mass. One way in which east Mediterranean cross-forms like those of the *Cathach* found their way about 500 to milieux in Ireland in which manuscripts were commonly written and art in other media produced is thus documented.

Manuscript comparanda for hands, texts and decorated initials in the *Cathach*

B. Schauman (1978) recognised two Irish hands among the four hands represented in manuscript S 45 sup. of the Ambrosian Library in Milan, a copy of Jerome's *Commentaria in Isaiam* (Commentary on the Book of Isaiah), a palimpsest whose primary script is a copy of the Gothic Bible translated by Ulfila, an Arian bishop. The manuscript bears the ex-libris of Atalanus, second abbot of Bobbio, until *c.* 625, and successor of that Italian monastery's founder, Columbanus. Schauman describes it as the earliest dated manuscript from Bobbio; these two Irish hands are thus the earliest datable samples of Irish script yet known. She compares the alphabet of her Irish Hand C with that of the *Cathach*, noting that both have the diminuendo feature, that the *ductus* of the letters is very similar and that both have wedge-shaped serifs. While both use variant forms of certain letters, these variants are used in different proportions. Schauman assesses the 'formality' of Hand C and the *Cathach* hand, describing formality as a measurement of the degree of letter contiguity in a hand: where all letters are contiguous, the hand is extremely informal, where all are separated, the hand is extremely formal. Of the two hands, the *Cathach* is the 'informal' one, with a script whose sources may have been cursive. In it she recognises 'the evolution of a decorous, stately Irish script…by the steadying of the characteristics of less stately scripts with which early Irish scribes must have been familiar' (Schauman 1978, 13). Hand C may illustrate a more advanced stage in this evolution; it and Schauman's other Irish Hand D are written in a more formal script than the *Cathach* and may claim a later date than it.

Schauman also considered the possibility that the differences between these hands derive from the separate scribal traditions of Iona and its *paruchia*, to which the *Cathach* belongs, and of Bangor, to which Columbanus belonged. The two Irish hands of this Bobbio manuscript (S 45 sup.) may therefore belong to a scribal tradition practised at Bangor before 590, when Columbanus left there on the *peregrinatio* that ended with his death at Bobbio in 615. If the *Cathach* can be considered earlier than the Bobbio manuscript, then we may be inclined to give more weight than before to the possibility that it belongs to the sixth century.

In an article in the *Gazette des Beaux-Arts*, Henry (1950) notes the characteristic deformation in Celtic style of the initials in the *Cathach* and a number of Bobbio manuscripts, principally the Orosius (Ambr. D 23 sup.) and the Commentary on the Book of Isaiah by Jerome (Ambr. S 45 sup.); she also notes the incorporation of Celtic motifs in these initials. The dot-contouring of the initials, as in the early sixth-century Vienna *Dioskorides*, together with the binding in quinions and the carpet page of D 23 sup., Henry ascribes to a Coptic origin; she compares the design of the carpet page of D 23 sup. with Coptic book covers now in New York and Vienna. The simplified fish found in the *Cathach* and incorporated as a double motif in an initial *N* in MS S 45 sup. she finds in Italian manuscripts of the fifth, sixth and seventh centuries as well as in Merovingian manuscripts. She quotes Lowe (CLA², 20, 41) as noting the Irish *G* of the *Cathach* as archaic and stating that the Irish calligraphic tradition at Bangor dates to 590, when Columbanus left Bangor, or earlier. Finally, she notes that in a poem on the rule of Bangor in the seventh century Antiphonary of Bangor (MS Ambr. C 5 inf.) there is a reference to *vinea vera / ex Aegypto transducta*, possibly an oblique reference to influences from the Coptic world (Henry 1950, 9, 14, 16–18, 20, 25, 30; 1965, 64–5).

In her recent edition of the text of Orosius's world history, M.-P. Arnaud-Lindet (1990) has designated the common ancestors of all existing manuscripts as α, β and γ, representing text-types of her Classes I, II and III respectively. The immediate exemplar of manuscripts F and H of Class I (α) may have been an Irish codex from Columbanus's Luxeuil, founded before 600. The earliest extant representative of Class II is B (Milan, Ambr. D 23 sup., from Bobbio), written in insular script like that of the *Cathach* and dating from the first half of the seventh century. It is a copy of an insular exemplar β´ and was taken to Bobbio from Ireland either in or shortly after the lifetime of Columbanus (died 615). Manuscripts M´ (Munich Clm. 29022, an eighth-century north Italian fragment), Q (Vat. Reg. lat. 296, written in the ninth century) and Δ (an abridgement of Orosius, probably written at Lorsch in the early ninth century) also descend from β´. Both α´ and β´, direct descendants of the archetypes of Classes I and II, are therefore associated with the Continental mission of Columbanus and thus derive, in one way or another, from the mother house, Bangor. The poor text in L (Florence, Bibl.

Laurentiana, Plut. 65, written in the sixth century and possibly connected with Ravenna), which is referred to above (Nordenfalk 1947), is a copy that branched off the main line of the archetype Class III (γ) and has left no descendants (Arnaud-Lindet 1990, lxxx-xc).

The *Cathach* was produced in an artistic milieu that was predominantly Irish La Tène in character. While the initials themselves and their filler motifs come from the Mediterranean, the ornamental early Christian motifs incorporated in them have a distinctive character: cross-forms, atrophied fishes and beasts and dot-contouring of the initials. Dot-contouring points to a source in Coptic contexts; the binding of manuscripts in quinions suggests an oriental source (CLA[1], vii). The cross-forms and their elaboration suggest a source in the east Mediterranean, from where distinctive pottery came to Ireland between 475 and 550. These distinctive forms are found together with marigolds on early metal ornaments and on stone carvings in early foundations throughout Ireland, from the non-Patrician province of the south-west as far north as County Down. Tradition ascribes this psalter to Colum Cille; palaeography (CLA[2], 41) and art allow the manuscript to be dated before 600. It is perhaps significant that Columbanus of Bangor and Bobbio had written an essay or treatise on the Psalms 'in elegant language' before 590, while he was still in Ireland, a copy of which was apparently taken to the continent (McNamara 1973, 222, 251–3).

Bible translations, Latin and Greek: the background to the *Cathach*

According to early tradition, the first translation of the Hebrew Pentateuch, or Law of Moses, was carried out at the behest of Pharaoh Ptolemy II Philadelphus (285–247 BC) and was into Greek. The Letter of Aristeas says that Ptolemy, at the suggestion of his librarian, dispatched an embassy to the high-priest Eleazar at Jerusalem, requesting him to send six elders from each of the twelve tribes of Israel to Alexandria, each bringing a scroll of the Law with him. Later tradition reduced this number from seventy-two to seventy, hence Septuagint (LXX). According to tradition, they completed their translations in seventy-two days. In another version, the translation was done during the reign of Ptolemy

Philometer (182–146 BC), probably with a view to encouraging the use of Greek among the Jews in his kingdom. The Septuagint is therefore the Alexandrian Greek version of the Old Testament, and the term, originally applied to the Greek translation of the Pentateuch, was later given to the entire translation. It appears that the earliest body of Greek translations was completed before 132 BC.

The Septuagint does not survive in its complete or pure form, and the existing Greek texts of some books or parts of books have been supplemented from other Greek versions. The first of these versions is by Aquila, a gentile who converted to Christianity and later to Judaism. He worked in the reign of the emperor Hadrian (AD 117–38), to whom he was related. His is a literal translation from the original Hebrew, even to the point of breaking with Greek idiom and syntax; this was well received by the Palestinian Jews, who had not approved of the Septuagint translation. The second version is by Theodotion, also a convert to Judaism, who wrote at the end of the second century AD. He revised the Septuagint against the standard Hebrew text that existed at the time and thus omitted material that had been added from other sources (for example to the Book of Daniel, the Greek text of which is longer than the Hebrew) and added material that had been omitted in the Septuagint translation, for example from the Book of Job. A third version was prepared by Symmachus (second century AD) after Theodotion. There exist fragments of three other anonymous translations, which were used by Origen (c. 185–254), mainly in his edition of the Psalms.

Origen, an Alexandrian Christian, endeavoured to restore the pure text of the Hebrew Old Testament, setting forth the text in six parallel columns—the Old Testament in Hebrew characters, the Hebrew text in Greek transcription, and the four Greek translations (the Septuagint and the three versions by Aquila, Theodotion and Symmachus). From its six-column layout it is known as the Hexapla. Origen recognised that the Greek contained clauses that were not in the Hebrew and omitted passages, some of them several chapters long, that the Hebrew contained. He edited the Greek Septuagint to conform with the Hebrew, correcting corruptions in the Septuagint that had been introduced from other manuscripts or other translations. To indicate where words or lines were missing in the Hebrew but present in the Greek he borrowed from Alexandrian philology the obelus (– or ÷); where words were wanting in the Septuagint but present in the Hebrew, he used the asterisk (*). These critical marks were later adopted by Jerome (347/8–420) for his revisions and translations from the Septuagint. Later writers, including Jerome, thought that Origen had restored the Septuagint, which had become the Greek text *par excellence* of the Church, to its pure form, and the text of the fifth column, the Hexaplaric Septuagint, was thereafter separately published. This formed the basis of Jerome's early revisions.

When Christianity spread into parts where Greek was not the common language, such as North Africa, Gaul and Italy, Latin translations were made of the Gospels and other parts of the New Testament, and, in particular, of the Psalms, which had become an integral part of the liturgy of the Church, as they were of the Jewish liturgy. Many such translations or part-translations proliferated, not all of them accurate, the text undergoing rapid and extensive development and differentiation. The Old Latin versions of the Old Testament, known as the *Vetus Latina*, survive only in fragments; almost all of the New Testament versions, because they were more prolific and more commonly used, survive. The African Church had a distinctive version of its own, known as the *Afra*, and Europe another, known as the *Itala*, of which there are several sub-forms. Eventually, so many versions existed that the situation became unmanageable and Jerome, exceptional in his time in having a knowledge of both Greek and Hebrew, was commissioned by Pope Damasus in 382 to prepare new and standard translations.

The first, published in 383, was a revision of good Latin texts of the four Gospels against a text of the Greek. Jerome states in his introduction that he made changes in the Latin only when the sense demanded it: the Gospel of Matthew was most heavily revised, that of John least. Jerome continued with further translations of groups of Old Testament books until 389, adding dedicatory epistles and historical and textual prefaces, only part of which survive. The Book of Psalms was revised twice: the first revision against the Old Latin is known as the *Romanum* (*c.* 384); the second, a more complete revision of the Old Latin against the Greek, based on the Hexapla, is known as the *Gallicanum* (*c.* 387). Both the preface and text of the *Gallicanum* survive intact (though not all of the asterisks and obeli as originally inserted by Jerome). In this Vulgate translation Jerome used the critical marks adopted by Origen, the asterisk denoting the parts of the Hebrew text omitted in the Greek of the Septuagint and the obelus marking those parts of the Septuagint not found in the Hebrew. In the preface to his correction (*Psalterium Romae dudum positus*), he asked future copyists to reproduce these critical signs along with the text itself. Jerome later abandoned the revision project in favour of a fresh translation of the Old Testament from the Hebrew, a restoration of the *Hebraica veritas*, where it still existed, and of the Aramaic where it did not (e.g. Books of Tobias and Judith). He began this translation project in 389 and continued until 405. His translation of the Psalms from the original Hebrew into Latin is known as the *Hebraicum*.

Jerome's translations were quickly corrupted by Old Latin readings where these were preferred, as they frequently were for centuries to come, so that his text of the Vulgate cannot now be recovered in its pure form. It seems clear from the evidence of the *Cathach* that the early Irish Church possessed the Psalms in both the Vulgate (*Gallicanum*) and *Hebraicum* texts.

The use of asterisk and obelus in the *Cathach*

As discussed in relation to other versions of the psalter above (pp 40–41), an asterisk indicates a passage or word in the Hebrew that is missing from the Greek, an obelus a passage or word missing from the Hebrew but found in the Greek. In the *Cathach*, the obeli can be palaeographically distinguished from the faint 'division signs' that were added in at the end of certain lines to mark verse or part-verse divisions (corresponding with the *stichoi* of the Greek text). The obeli are larger than the division signs, are in the same ink as the main text and were copied at the same time as it.

There are twenty-five uses of the obelus (Fig. 18) in the *Cathach*, indicating omissions from the Hebrew. Four of these (at Psalms 89:17b; 91:10a; 94:9c; 97:5) are placed before words that are in Jerome's *Hebraicum* but are missing from the Irish family of this translation, represented in the manuscript group AKI (comprising the Codex Amiatinus, Florence, dated *ante* 716; Karlsruhe Cod. Aug. XXXVIII, ninth century; and the Psalter of

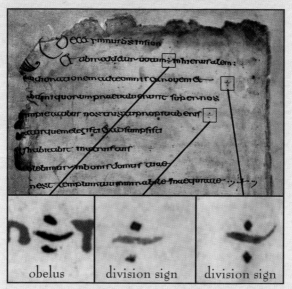

Fig. 18—Fol. 25v of *Cathach*, showing obelus and division signs.

St Ouen (siglum **I**), tenth century, the oldest and purest text of the three) and others. They therefore represent not Jerome's original *Hebraicum* but a revision of the *Gallicanum* against the Irish *Hebraicum*, indicating words missing from or altered in the (Irish) *Hebraicum* but present in the *Gallicanum*. In two places, the obeli are misplaced, at Psalm 84:12a, where ÷ *et veritas* is not omitted in either the Hebrew, Greek or Latin, and at Psalm 104:44a, *in laetitia* ÷ *et dedit illis*, where the obelus should have been placed before the *et* at the beginning of the verse (÷ *et electos suos in laetitia*...), where there is an omission in the *Hebraicum*. The omission of ÷ *et in bracchio* (Psalm 88:11b) represents a variant of the Gallican Vulgate found in the *Cathach* and in the Psalter of St Ouen (MS Rouen, Bibl. Mun. 24). The rest of the obeli represent omissions from the established *Hebraicum*. The presence of corrections from the Irish family of the *Hebraicum* can be explained in two ways: (i) the Irish schools had a text of Jerome's *Hebraicum* peculiar to themselves at some indeterminate time before the *Cathach* was written; (ii) they had compared the text of the *Gallicanum* against that of the *Hebraicum* in order to present in a single text the results of both of Jerome's critical translations. This collation was present in the exemplar of the *Cathach* also; the exemplar may even have been a double psalter, with the *Gallicanum* and *Hebraicum* on alternate pages, of which the *Cathach* scribe copied only the *Gallicanum*. This indicates that a certain amount of early critical-textual work on the psalter was being done in the Irish schools, in McNamara's (1973, 267) opinion 'at a very early date in the sixth century at the latest'. Just how much was done, and what the methodology of these sixth-century scholars was, remain to be explored. Certainly the Irish knew the purpose of these critical signs, apart from merely copying them from their sources: this is evident from, among other sources, the Treatise on the Psalter in Old Irish (thought to be eighth century) and from the letter of the anonymous Irishman in Milan on the emendation of the Latin psalter against the Greek (ninth century) (McNamara 1973, 229–30, 235–7). There is therefore method and purpose behind the use of these signs in the *Cathach*.

There are twenty-two uses of the asterisk (Fig. 19) in the *Cathach*. One (Psalm 53:3b) was written by the scribe over an erasure, and three were entered as editorial restorations in the now mutilated fragment (Psalms 58:6a; 73:15b; 92:3c). Nine of the twenty-two asterisks correspond to Jerome's original Gallican text. Five further asterisks occur in places where there are words in the Hebrew that are not in the Greek; these are correctly under asterisk even though they are absent in the text of Jerome's *Gallicanum* as we have it. One of the five, at Psalm 34:20b, may have had an asterisk in Jerome's original *Gallicanum*; the remaining four (Psalms 53:5c; 70:8a; 77:21a; 88:45b) represent additions in the Irish *Gallicanum*. With the exception of Psalm 77:21a, all of these variants also have Greek, Syriac and/or Old Latin support. A further asterisk at Psalm 85:12a represents an omission in some manuscripts of one branch of the Greek text.

The remaining seven asterisks are placed against passages that are in the Greek. Five of them are placed against words present in all texts of the psalter—the Hebrew, the Greek, the Old Latin and the *Gallicanum*. Two of them can readily be explained: the omission of *et* in Psalm 49:7 (*Israhel * et*) may be a misplacement of the asterisk before the word preceding *Israhel, tibi*, which is omitted in several Greek and Latin sources. Similarly, in Psalm 103:7 *tonitrui * tui* is an error by the scribe, since *tui* is an omission from three Irish manuscripts of the *Hebraicum* (group RAK—R being the eighth-century Codex Reginensis; A and K as above) and should therefore be marked with an obelus. The other five (Psalms 34:15a; 53:3b; 58:6a; 65:7a; 85:4b) do not at present permit any explanation, unless they are simply errors.

Our present 'accepted' text of the Septuagint Greek psalter (Rahlfs 1979) is a reconstruction from the extant witnesses: there is no reason to assume that the Greek from which the text of the *Cathach* is ultimately derived was identical with it, and the possibility that the ancestral text of the *Cathach* was not simply a text of the 'pure' *Gallicanum* but a particular text of the Greek against which the *Gallicanum* was compared should be examined. There are also other possible explanations for these anomalies in the use of asterisk and obelus, e.g. copying errors or misplacements resulting from the simultaneous collation of two (or even more) versions of the Latin psalter.

Fig. 19—Fol. 19r of *Cathach*, showing rubric and asterisk.

The rubrics in the *Cathach* and what they contain

The rubrics, or headings (see illustration above), were added by the *prima manus* in orange ink above the text of each psalm proper in a more uncial hand after the main text was written. In some cases the scribe left insufficient room, so that a word or phrase occasionally had to be disposed in the margins. This technique of adding rubricated headings in spaces left for them in the main text can also be found in Egyptian (Coptic) illumination.

They were clearly not added to the *Cathach* as an *aide memoire*, since the ancients learned the psalter by heart, and psalmody was not done with a book (Dyer 1989; Woolfenden 1993). The *Cathach* was probably kept for private reading and study or as a special possession. We do not know if it was used for communal monastic service.

Each psalm in the *Cathach* has a tripartite heading giving, where they have been copied or are fully preserved, (i) a heading proper (verse 1 of each psalm, from the Greek text, the Septuagint), (ii) what has been taken by Lawlor, Salmon and others as some liturgical instruction (e.g. Psalm 47: *legendus ad Apocalipsim Iohannis*) but is more probably a devotional directive (Dyer 1989, 69–70), and (iii) an interpretative heading or *titulus*. Several such series of headings, deriving from different Fathers, were identified and edited by Dom Pierre Salmon (Salmon 1959; 1962). The series of *tituli* in the *Cathach* is the oldest, and the *Cathach*, being the second oldest Latin psalter now in existence, is also the earliest representative of that series, designated Series I. Only the devotional/liturgical headings, where they are present, and the *tituli* proper were edited by Dom Salmon (Salmon 1959, 48–74). He identified six series: with the exception of Series I, they can all be quite readily dated and their source(s) identified. Series IV derives from the psalm commentary of Eusebius of Caesarea (*c.* 265–339) and is found in the famous Greek Codex Alexandrinus (fifth century); it survives in an Old Latin translation that first appears in Carolingian psalters of the eighth to ninth century. Series III derives from the homilies of Origen of Alexandria (*c.* 185–254) on the psalms in the translation of Jerome. Series V and II are of fourth- and fifth-century derivation respectively. The most recent series is VI, which derives from Cassiodorus (*c.* 485–580), later adapted by Bede (673–735). These series were thus composed between the end of the third and the end of the sixth century. The authors of the Series IV and VI, Eusebius and Cassiodorus, are known. Although we know the ultimate sources of the other series, we do not know the circumstances of their composition or early dissemination. The oldest texts are the most concise, the later series more elaborate and wordy. All the ancient psalters, Latin and Greek, contain this material, whether in the form of collective summaries or as rubrics before each individual psalm, as they appear in the *Cathach*. Their purpose, as Dom Salmon has pointed out, is to orient prayer and to facilitate interpretation, that is, to identify the speaker or *persona* of each psalm and give it a coherent interpretation.

For the Church of the martyrs and the early Fathers, the psalter was a book about Christ, and each psalm was either *vox de Christo*, *vox ecclesiae ad Christum* or *vox Christi ad Patrem*. The Christological interpretation of the psalms, i.e. the interpretation of them as referring to Christ or the events of his life, can first be found in the citations from them in the Acts of the Apostles and in the Book of Hebrews in the New Testament, e.g. the use of Psalm 16:10 in Acts 2:27, Psalm 2:7 in Hebrews 1:5 and Psalm 8:5–7 in Hebrews 2:6–8. This mode of interpretation was continued thereafter by Justin Martyr, Irenaeus, Clemens of Alexandria and most of the major Greek Fathers (Linton 1961). The Christological series found in the *Cathach* is doubly valuable, since its roots are in early Christianity and the *Cathach* is the earliest known manuscript witness to it. Its sources have not been identified, and most modern authorities are content to state that it is not possible to determine whether it is native or transmitted to Ireland. The sources are certainly not Latin, although there are tenuous connections with Tertullian and Augustine. Dom Salmon (1959, 53) has noted the close correspondence between the interpretative heading to Psalm 1, *De Joseph dicit qui corpus Christi sepelivit* (defective in the *Cathach*), and the exegesis of Tertullian as well as some similarities with the exegesis of Augustine in Psalms 48, 50, 56, 60, 86, 90 and 115. There are Christological elements in both Jerome's Shorter Commentaries on the Psalms (*Commentarioli in Psalmos*) and Augustine's great commentary, but they are quite different from the *Cathach tituli*, which do not conform to the interpretative headings given by either. It can now be shown that Dom Salmon's assertion, 'Certain elements of these series, especially of the first one, may go back to the third century' (Salmon 1962, 51), has some truth and that the *tituli* of Series I bear a striking similarity to some Greek psalm commentaries.

Although the rubrics of Series I can be separated into three parts, there is no manuscript evidence that these three elements circulated separately. Also, in the *Cathach* at least, the three headings clearly form an integrated text. Unfortunately, because of the fragmentary and poor preservation of the *Cathach*, and partly because of scribal errors, many of these headings are now missing, corruptly or incompletely preserved or illegible.

The first element, the *titulus* of each psalm, being the first verse, was taken from the Septuagint into Jerome's critical revision against it, the *Gallicanum*. The text of the *Cathach tituli* differs in some respects from the *tituli* of the critical *Gallicanum* in the Vatican and Stuttgart editions and agrees more closely with those of Eusebius of Caesarea and other Greek Fathers. The second element, the devotional rubric (*legendus ad…*), may in some cases also derive from the same source(s) that provided the *inscriptiones*, or headings, and the *tituli*. For example, Eusebius's exegesis of Psalm 44:10–16 is suggestive of the devotional rubric in the *Cathach*, *Legendus ad evangelium Mathei de regina austri* (cf. Matthew 11:42, Luke 11:31). Also, Eusebius's and Athanasius's exegeses of Psalm 68:1 (as well as the text of the psalm itself, of course) bear a very close affinity to the *Cathach titulus*, *Legendus ad lectionem Jonae prophetae…vox Christi cum pateretur*: the psalm is associated with a reading from the prophet Jonah (probably chapter 2, Jonah's prayer of affliction in the belly of the whale), and the *vox* of the psalm is that of Christ in his suffering. The *titulus* can certainly be recovered from the exegesis of these Fathers, and the devotional link is clearly suggested in some texts. Similarly, Eusebius's exegesis of Psalm 47 suggests its association with Apocalypse 21, on the vision of the New Jerusalem.

The third element is of most interest in determining the textual antecedents of the *Cathach*. Dom Salmon (1962, 51–4) has shown that the *Cathach* series is the source from which all the other witnesses to Series I derive, via its transmission to England in the seventh century. The subsequent history of the series is of little interest in this context but has been studied in some detail by Lawlor (1916, 413–35) and amplified by Salmon (1962, 51–4). The series is designated Christological, that is the *persona*, where identified, is denoted *propheta* and the *voces*, or addresses, of the psalms are in almost all cases attributed to Christ, the apostles or the Church. To give a rather intricate example, Psalm 44, slightly corrupt in the *Cathach*, reads: *Propheta pro patre de Christo et ecclesia dicit*, that is, the psalm is to be interpreted as the words of the Father, through the prophet, to or of Christ and the Church, specifically of the Church called from among the Gentiles.

In fact, the majority of the *tituli* bear some similarity to the exegesis of Eusebius of Caesarea (*c.* 265–339) (PG 23, 441C–1221C) and to that of Athanasius of Alexandria (295–373) (PG 27, 60C–545C), whose dependence on the exegesis of Eusebius (Rondeau 1958; Vian 1991, 16) and, to a lesser extent, on the exegesis of Gregory of Nyssa (died 394) has been demonstrated (McDonough 1962; Heine 1995). Eusebius's vast commentary is based upon the Hexaplaric text and the commentaries of his mentor, Origen of Alexandria, to which he had direct access; both commentaries survive only in fragments. Eusebius gives the historical or literal exegesis of each psalm as well as its metaphorical interpretation, with some explanation of the *voces* and *personae* of the psalm. The *Cathach tituli* refer to the sense of the psalm as a whole or to a specific verse in it and are terse to the point of obscurity. The commentaries, however, being extended exegeses of the psalms, do not always convey the substance of the *titulus* at the beginning, where one might expect to find it. Instead, this information is sometimes diffused throughout the text and at other times conveyed within the exegesis of a specific verse or phrase of the psalm. Athanasius is much more succinct in his exposition than Eusebius and is therefore easier to use as a source. Eusebius's exegesis is both Alexandrian and Antiochean, that is both allegorical and historical, although it leans toward the former. The commentary of Athanasius, the great representative of the Alexandrian school of exegesis, is distinctly allegorical.

There is no extant translation of Eusebius's commentary, although Jerome, who cannot always be relied on, states that Eusebius of Vercelli made a translation of it into Latin in the fourth century (*De uiris illustribus*, §96). There is evidence that Hilary of Poitiers (*c.* 310–367/8) was familiar with parts of Eusebius's commentary (especially Psalms 1:65 and 188) and may have translated it, although his own exegesis, especially *Tractatus super Psalmos*, mainly relies on the now very fragmentary commentaries of Origen. It is certainly possible that the text of one or other of these translations was known in the Irish schools or that an ancient Latin psalter containing headings derived from Eusebius's commentary reached Ireland. However, in the complete absence of any trace of those translations it is not possible to make definitive statements. Some of the *Cathach* series of headings may very well be the product of an indigenous

Irish tradition of psalm interpretation based on careful study of Scripture, of which there is ample evidence from the early Irish monastic schools. It is not likely that all of them are the product of native invention, independent of any outside influence or source. The links with the commentaries of Eusebius, Athanasius and Gregory are almost certainly not direct, but some connection with the Alexandrian tradition of exegesis seems quite possible given the proven patristic derivation of the other five series and in the absence of any provable dependence upon the Latin Fathers.

The sources of some of the headings remain unidentified. The *titulus* to Psalm 64, *vox ecclesiae ante baptismum paschalismatum*, is particularly unusual. The hapax or unique occurrence of the word '*paschalismatum*' is a loan translation from Greek, being a neuter Latin adjective derived from πασχαλισμός. The *titulus* may have liturgical significance (Salmon 1959, 52) or it may refer to the 'baptism' of the Church in Christ's blood, his passion. A fuller investigation of the *tituli* and their sources would greatly help our understanding of their tripartite structure (where it exists) and text. They were almost certainly transmitted together as a unit from an ancient psalter that underwent refinements and additions from native tradition.

The language of the *tituli* has a number of peculiarities that may indicate some dependence on a Greek source, especially the use of the Graecisms *exomologessem* in Psalm 43 (*ex homo legessem* in the *Cathach*) and *paschalismatum* in Psalm 64 (only a fragment of the word is visible in the *Cathach*). The peculiarities of the syntax and language deserve comment—for example, the *titulus* to Psalm 35, *Profeta cum laude opera ipsius Iudae dicit,* and the strange phraseology of Psalm 36, *...monet ad fidei firmamentum*. Salmon also noted these peculiarities but took them to be liturgical elements in the headings. The liturgical heading to Psalm 26, *Legendus ad lectionem Esaiae prophetae: ecce qui serviunt tibi bona manducabunt* (Isaiah 65:13 paraphrased from the Old Latin; defective in the *Cathach*), would lead one to suspect that the Old and New Testament readings for use or meditation in conjunction with each psalm were of the Old Latin type. There are similarities here with the bilingual Easter Vigil lections and the forty short readings from the Minor Prophets in the codex known as *Liber Commonei* (Oxford, Bodleian Library, MS Auct. F.4./32, dated 817): the Latin texts in this ancient collection have a peculiar phraseology that is indicative of their accommodation to a Greek original, and are distinctly pre-Vulgate in type (Fischer 1952; Hunt 1961; Lapidge 1983; Breen 1992).

Several examples of correspondence between the *Cathach* and the commentaries of Eusebius, Athanasius and/or Gregory have been isolated. A systematic examination of other patristic commentaries that are likely to bear some relationship to the *Cathach* series—such as those of Hesychius of Jerusalem, Didymus of Alexandria or Diodore of Tarsus—has not been made, nor has the content of every *titulus* in the *Cathach*, ending at Psalm 105, been examined. Further research would undoubtedly bring to light many more correspondences. The following are a few examples, chosen for their brevity and clarity from a longer list, as illustrations of close similarity with the commentaries of each of the three Fathers Eusebius, Athanasius and Gregory. All citations from patristic sources are given in the modern Latin translation in Migne (PG) to facilitate direct comparison with the *Cathach*. The Greek original has not been quoted, except for the purpose of illustration.

Recent researches by McNamara (1998; 1999) have indicated plausible similarities between the *Cathach* series and other Latin Psalm commentaries, including the early seventh-century *Glosa Psalmorum ex traditione Seniorum*, but they demonstrate no direct dependence either way. The source(s) from which the *Cathach* derived its *tituli* series can certainly be placed well within the sixth century, earlier than any of the comparanda adduced from later medieval Latin tradition. Suggestive verbal coincidences indicated by McNamara between the texts of the individual psalms and their headings in the *Cathach* series only show that the series was informed at source by the exegesis of the psalms, which is no more than what one would expect. It does not prove that this series, alone of the six, was *sui generis*. The question of its dependence upon a Greek source therefore remains a plausible hypothesis.

The sources of the *tituli* in the *Cathach*

In the following, *Cathach* headings are represented in bold typeface (with spelling following Lawlor's transcription); underlining represents the author's highlighting of similarities between the *Cathach* headings and the commentaries of the Fathers; direct quotations from the Bible cited by the Fathers in their commentaries are placed between quotation marks. The figures in parentheses immediately preceding quotations from commentaries of Athanasius, Eusebius or Gregory refer to the volume and column numbers in Migne (PG); volume and column numbers are separated by a semicolon.

(1) Psalm 32:1—**Psalmus Dauid. profeta cum laude dei populum hortatur**

Athanasius, *Expositio in Psalmos*, at Psalm 32: 1 (PG 27; 163/4)—In presenti docet eos qui jam in Christum crediderunt laudare Dominum suum

The *Cathach* heading means 'the prophet exhorts the people with [or to] the praise of God', and Athanasius interprets it similarly.[9]

(2) Psalm 34:1—**Huic Dauid. uox Christi in passione de Iudaeis dicit**

Athanasius, *Expositio in Psalmos*, at Psalm 34:1 (PG 27; 169/70)—Inducitur item persona Christi ea ennarantis quae sibi tempore Passionis a Iudaeis illata sunt mala

The psalm begins 'Judge thou O Lord them that wrong me'. The *Cathach titulus* and Athanasius are in complete agreement: the voice of Christ in his Passion speaks of the wrongs committed against him by the Jews.

(3) Psalm 35:1—**profeta cum laude opera ipsius Iudae dicit**

This heading, inserted by Lawlor from manuscripts ABRS (cf. Lawlor 1916, 242–3, for key to manuscripts) is no longer present in the *Cathach*; its absence is noted in Salmon's apparatus

---

[9] The translations of *Cathach* headings in this booklet are Aidan Breen's. Readers should note that the headings in the English version of the psalms on the CD-ROM do not necessarily match those in the *Cathach*; in particular, the English version (Challoner's edition of the Douay-Rheims translation) does not always include details of the *persona* or *voces* of the respective psalms.

criticus (Salmon 1959, 59). The heading, despite the preponderance of MS witnesses to it, may be somewhat corrupt. Two MSS (Vat. lat. 84 and Vat. lat. 12985) add a following phrase, construing the psalm as a prophetic accusation against the Jewish people (*ejusque est accusatio de populo judaico*; cf. Series II). Athanasius's exegesis is very similar to both of these:

Athanasius, *Expositio in Psalmos,* at Psalm 35:1 (PG 27; 173/6)—<u>Superbiae Judaici populi accusationem continet hic Psalmus</u>...<u>atque justa Dei judicia decantat, quod orbem condiderit. Ad haec etiam gratiarum actionem Patri offert pro beneficiis per Jesum collatis</u>... 'Iniquitatem meditatus est in cubiculo suo...' (Psalm 35:5) <u>Vigiles et insomnes noctes eorum qui Christo insidias parabant significat</u>... Judaei enim mysterium per leges et prophetas edocti exciderunt, gentes vero...assumptae sunt...

The correct translation of the Latin might be: 'the prophet speaks with praise of His [i.e. God's] works to Juda [i.e. the Jewish people, or Judas the traitor].'

(4) Psalm 39:1—**patientia populi est**
Athanasius, *Expositio in Psalmos,* Psalm 39:2 (PG 27; 189/90)—<u>Refertur canticum ex persona novi populi</u> de lacu miseriae reducti... Expectans expectavi Dominum, et intendit mihi (Psalm 39:2). Simile huic: '<u>In patientia vestra possidebitis animas vestras</u>' (Luke 21:19).

Athanasius cites the text 'in your <u>patience</u> shall you possess your souls' as a proof of the meaning of the psalm; the persona is that of the <u>new people</u> of the Word (ἐκ προσώπου τοῦ νέου λαοῦ).

(5) Psalm 43:1—**hic ex homo legessem[10] legendus ad epistolam Pauli ad Romanos. profeta ad dominum de operibus eius paenitentiam gerens pro populo Iudaico**
Eusebius, *Commentarii in Psalmos*, at Psalm 43 (PG 23; 383/6)—<u>nimirum de ruina Judaici populi, ex prophetarum</u>

---

[10] for ex homo legessem *read* exomolegesim.

persona a filiis Core prolatae... In superioribus itaque lacryma-
bantur, doloremque suum Deo renuntiabant; in presenti vero
ipsas calamitates ennarant... 'Deum celebrabimus tota die, et
nomini tuo confitebimur in aeternum' (Psalm 43:9).
Confessionem (ἐξομολόγησιν) porro pro gratiarum actione
usurpare Scripturae solent... Sed haec quidem ex persona chori
prophetici dicta sunt. Quae vero deinde feruntur iidem rursus,
multitudinis casus sibi ascribentes, ennarant... Quoniam
multitudo totius populi Judaici, in omni impietatis et improbitatis
genere volutata, non aliena erat a corpore prophetarum, populi
aerumnas sibi proprias attribuentes...Haec tam multa chorus
propheticus in sua ad Deum supplicatione, calamitates populi
ascribens sibi, prosecutus est.

Athanasius, *Expositio in Psalmos,* Psalm 43:18 (PG 27;
205/6)—'haec omnia venerunt...' (Psalm 43:18) Jam diximus
prophetas esse qui ex populi persona supplicationes offerunt,
quasi propria sibi reputantes mala ipsi peccatorum causa
obvenientia.

The words of the psalm are those of the prophet(s) to God,
attributing to themselves the tribulations and calamities which
have befallen the Jewish people.

(6) Psalm 44:1—**legendus ad euangelium Mathei de regina
austri. profeta ad** [Salmon reads **pro**] **patre de Christo et
ecclesia dicit**
Eusebius, *Commentarii in Psalmos,* at Psalm 68 (PG 23;
721/2)—Quadragesimus itaque quartus de Dilecto prophetiam,
atque gentium Ecclesiae a pejoribus ad meliora immutationem,
complectitur...
and again at Psalm 44 (PG 23; 391/394)—ut intelligamus
totam sermonis seriem canticum pro Dilecto complecti; aut...
'Canticum in Dilectum' (Psalm 44:1)... Dilectum autem illum
esse Unigenitum Dei Filium... 'Dominus dabit Verbum
evangelizantibus virtute multa. Rex virtutum Dilecti' (Psalm
67:12–13); ubi aperte ac speciatim Dominus Deus universorum
memoratur (Σαφῶς δὲ κανταῦθα ἰδίως μνημονευομένου
Κυρίου τοῦ Θεοῦ τῶν ὅλων); ac rursum speciatim Dilectus, ac
demum tertio ordine, evangelizantes Dilectum, quibus ab ipso
Deo Verbum dari...Hic adjiciatur ad sermonem totum

obsignandum, salutare Evangelium paterna voce Dilectum apud homines clamore edito commonstrasse: 'Hic est Filius meus dilectus, in quo mihi complacui' (Matthew 17:5). Tot tantisque de Dilecto prolatis, plane demum ac sine contradictione fuerit haec prophetia in titulo sic enuntiata: 'Canticum pro Dilecto' (Psalm 44:1). Quod autem hic ipse Christus, alius ab eo, qui ipsum iniunxit Patre, in eodem Psalmo postea declaratur... Quidam arbitrati sunt ex persona Patris Psalmum sive canticum pronuntiari de Verbo... <u>Mihi porro haec ad propheticum chorum referenda videntur.</u>

Athanasius, *Expositio in Psalmos*, Psalm 44:1 (PG 27; 207/14)—Praesens canticum David offert, scilicet Christo... 'Eructavit cor meum verbum bonum' (Psalm 44:2). Hoc Pater ait de Filio: genitus namque est Deus ex Deo.

Eusebius (PG 23; 951) isolates the three elements in the *titulus* of this psalm: (i) that it is a prophecy expressed through David (cf. also Athanasius), (ii) that it is in the 'voice', or on behalf of the Father (cf. also Athanasius), and (iii) that it relates to Christ and the calling of the Church from the gentiles. The *persona* of the psalm is not God the Father but the prophet. The early Church interpreted this psalm as messianic: Psalm 44:7–8 (Sedis tua Deus in saeculum saeculi virga directionis virga regni tui. Dilexisti iustitiam et odisti iniquitatem. Proptera unxit te Deus Deus tuus oleo laetitiae prae consortibus tuis.) is taken to refer to Christ in Hebrews 1:8–9. This is also the understanding of the *Cathach* heading.

(7) Psalm 52:1—**In finem pro Melech intelligentia Dauid legendus ad euangelium Mathei. increpat Iudeos incredulos operibus negantes deum**

Gregory of Nyssa, *In inscriptiones Psalmorum*, at Psalm 52 (PG 44; 566)—'inutiles facti sunt omnes' (Psalm 52:4)... Dominus igitur propter haec 'de caelo respexit super filios hominum' (Psalm 52:2). <u>Quae verba Domini inter homines conversationem indicant, quando praeeuntes ad incredulitatem sacerdotes et Pharisaeos, et Scribas, omnes subditi secuti sunt: illi enim erant, qui blasphemis suis dentibus populum laniabant et devorabant.</u>

The Lord rebukes the unbelieving Jews, especially the priests, Pharisees and Scribes, who by their deeds deny God and with their blasphemies destroy the people.

(8) Psalm 54:1—**In finem intellectus in carminibus Dauid. uox Christi aduersus magnatos Iudeorum et de Iuda traditore**

Eusebius, *Commentarii in Psalmos*, Psalm 54:13–14 (PG 23; 474)—Ex quibus omnibus aestimo non posse ad Davidis personam haec referri; sed prophetica vi arbitror dicta esse, et in uno Salvatore et Domino nostro completa, quando Judaicae gentis principes, Hierosolymae in unum congregati, consessum ac consilium inierunt, quomodo eum perderent. (Ἐξ ὧν ἁπάντων ἡγοῦμαι μὴ χώραν ἔχειν ἀναφέρεσθαι τὰ προκείμενα ἐπί τὸ τοῦ Δαυιδ πρόσωπον· προφητικῇ δέ οἶμαι δυνάμει λελέχθαι αὐτά, καὶ ἐπὶ μόνον τὸν Σωτῆρα καὶ Κύριον ἡμῶν συνίστασθαι πεπληρωμένα, ὅτε, κατὰ τὸ αὐτὸ συναχθέντές οἱ τοῦ Ἰουδαίων ἔθνοῦς ἀρχοντές ἐπὶ τῆς Ἱερουσαλὴμ, συνέδριον εποιήσαντο καὶ σκέψιν ὅπῶς αὐτόν ἀπολέσωσιν· ἐν ᾧ οἱ μὲν θάνατον αὐτοῦ κατεψηφίσαντο)...Aperte porro Evangelii scriptura prophetiam asserit, haec de proditore Juda accipiens, (ἐπὶ τὸν προδότην Ἰούδαν ἐκλαβοῦσα τὸ) 'Si inimicus meus maledixisset mihi, sustinuissem utique...' (Psalm 54:13)

The words of the Psalm inveigh against the great ones of the Jewish people when they conspired to do away with Christ, and against Judas the traitor.

(9) Psalm 57:1—**In finem ne disperdas Dauid. In tituli inscriptione profeta denioribus [*lege*: de senioribus] Iudaeorum dicit**.

Eusebius, *Commentarii in Psalmos*, at Psalm 57:7 (PG 23; 531/2)—Animadvertendum autem est, num prophetia isthaec, quae tota cohaeret et una serie jungitur cum praecedentibus, finem describat eorum, qui prophetias de Christo meditantur, justitiam ore loquuntur, et venientem ipsum receperunt; neque tamen vocem eius audierunt qua clamabat ipsis haec dicens: 'Qui habet aures audiendi audiat' (Mt. 11:5): qui sese serpenti similes effecerunt, et aures sibi pararunt 'sicut aspides surdae et obturantis aures suas' (Psalm 57:5). Ii vero ipsi dentes suos molasque suas blasphemis in Salvatorem nostrum dictis exacuerunt ...(Οι δὲ αὐτοι καὶ τοῦ ' ὀδόντας αὐτῶν καὶ τας μύλας διὰ τῶν κατὰ τοῦ Σωτῆρος ἡμῶν βλασφημιῶν ἠκόνησαν)...Possunt item haec dici de omnibus qui athea dogmata, et impias falsasque sententias in atheis heresibus consarcinarunt, atque de iis qui sapientiam huius saeculi profitentur, qui linguas suas contra salutarem doctrinam exacuerunt.

Eusebius implicitly equates those who blaspheme the Lord with the Elders of Israel.

/ (10) Ps 58:1—**vox Christi de Iudeis ad patrem**
Eusebius, *Commentarii in Psalmos*, at Psalm 58 (PG 23; 537/8C)—Exsurge in occursum meum, et vide. Deinde vero, tanta usus fiducia, a prophetico spiritu illustratur, ac ediscit futurum tempus, quo ipse Christus Dei vexationibus et insidiis Judaici populi impetetur, ac servator et inspector universarum gentium erit.

(φωτίζεται ὑπό τοῦ προφητικοῦ πνεύματος, καὶ διδάσκεται, ὡς ἄρα ἔσται τις καιρὸς ἐν ᾧ καὶ ὁ Χριστὸς τοῦ θεοῦ διωχθήσεται, καὶ ἐπιδουλευθήσεται ὑπὸ τοῦ Ἰουδαίων ἔθνους, σωτήρ τε καὶ ἐπίσκοπος τῶν ἐθνῶν ἀπάντων γενήσεται)

(11) Psalm 68:1—**legendus ad lectionem Ionae profetae et ad euangelium Iohannis. vox Christi cum pateretur**
Athanasius, *Expositio in Psalmos*, Psalm 68:15–16 (PG 27; 305/6)—Continet psalmus precationem Salvatoris, ex persona humanitatis oblatam, et narrat quae causae fuerint quod ei mortem crucis obtulerint. Insuper ipsam passionem clare narrat... 'Libera me ab iis qui oderunt me et de profundis aquarum' et 'Non me demergat tempestas aquae' (Psalm 53:15–16).

Eusebius, *Commentarii in Psalmos*, at Psalm 68 (PG 23, 723/4)—Quare dixeris prophetiam esse ex persona Servatoris nostri enarrantis ea quae sibi postea contigerunt; praedictionemque eorum quae Judaeis post tantos ausus illata sunt. Orditur itaque Servator orationem emittens ad Patrem his verbis:

'Salvum me fac, Deus, quoniam intraverunt aquae usque ad animam meam' (Psalm 68:2) .... Ipse igitur quem non alium esse quam Dei Verbum superius demonstravimus, orationem effundit ad Patrem, hominis quem assumpsit cruciatus sibi proprios reputans, quare ait: 'Salvum me fac, Deus, quoniam intraverunt aquae usque ad animam meam. Infixus sum in limo profundi, et non est substantia. Veni in altitudinem maris, et tempestas demersit me' (Psalm 68:2–3).

Both exegeses interpret the Psalm as the words of Christ on his passion, spoken prophetically through David. The association with the story of Jonah is implicit from the reference to drowning in the watery depths.

Some provisional conclusions can be drawn from the above examples:

1. The series of *tituli* exemplified in the *Cathach* bears a strong relation to the psalm exegesis of some of the Greek Fathers, especially Eusebius of Caesarea, Athanasius and probably— but to a lesser extent—Gregory of Nyssa. Direct dependence on any one of these commentaries cannot be sustained, for two reasons. Firstly, because (to my knowledge) we have no Greek series of *tituli* to compare directly with the *Cathach* or other cognate Latin MS witnesses, and so we lack comparative textual evidence on which to base a firmer hypothesis. Secondly, several of the *Cathach* headings have not yet been traced, not even the source of Psalm 64, with its rare Greek word *paschalismos*. Since there is nothing comparable in the Greek sources so far examined for a number of the *tituli*, clearly not all the sources or, more precisely, all the congeners of the series have been traced. The imperfections in our extant manuscript sources must also be taken into account. With the exception of Gregory's *De titulis Psalmorum*, of which a critical edition has recently been published (Heine 1995), the enormous commentaries of Eusebius, Athanasius and others are still only available in imperfect early editions, reprinted in PG (Migne). The headings in the *Cathach* were copied, sometimes inaccurately, from an Irish exemplar, and it is quite evident that this exemplar had in turn taken them from its exemplar. In each case, therefore, we are working at several removes from the

original documents; we must therefore take care not to make hasty inferences.

2. If the parallels with the Greek texts so far scrutinised are merely a coincidence in interpretative tradition, one must nonetheless explain the evident Graecisms of syntax and vocabulary in the *tituli* in some other way and dismiss as purely coincidental the close similarities in thought and even vocabulary between the *Cathach* series and the Greek texts. This is not to dismiss or minimise the evidence that the liturgical rubrics and *tituli* might be the product of a living tradition of exegesis in early medieval lreland. The sources, Latin and Greek, of the other series of *tituli* have been identified. No doubt such series were later modified and added to (and many are confused with each other in the manuscripts), but they were not manufactured *ex nihilo*, and they clearly belong to an ancient and continuous Christian tradition of giving specificChristological interpretations to many of the psalms.

3. The full three-part headings in the *Cathach* are almost certainly the product of a tradition of exegesis and not the work of an isolated scholar. Whether that tradition is entirely indigenous or relied upon imported material—the latter being far more probable at this very early period—cannot be established. It does seem likely, however, that the series was transmitted to the Western Church intact, probably in an ancient psalter, and thence to Ireland at a very early date, in the fifth or early sixth century. The tradition of exegesis is also witnessed in later Irish exegetical material on the psalms. If the psalms of this series were composed in Ireland, it is hard to believe that a school of Irish biblical scholars chanced quite coincidentally upon interpretative headings so similar, for the entire range of the psalms, to those in the sources that we have examined. If the original source(s) of the series is/are Greek, this merely adds to the growing body of evidence in support of the transmission of liturgical and other materials of Greek origin (like bodies of *onomastica sacra* and possibly a number of patristic texts) to Ireland from diverse locations. These materials were then preserved in Latin form in the host country.

Conclusions

Elements of the both the ornament and the codicology of the *Cathach* point to influence from early Christian sources in the eastern Mediterranean. Specifically, the cross-forms indicate influence from the non-Latin provinces of the late Roman Empire in that part of the Mediterranean within the late fifth and early sixth centuries. Examination of the codicology suggests that these artistic influences are mirrored in the distinctive traces of Greek derivation in the verse structure and in other features revealed by the exegesis of the psalm *tituli*, which, though now imperfectly preserved within the manuscript, appear to derive ultimately from the Alexandrian Church. The authors, arguing from very different sets of material, reinforce the opinions of Lowe, Schauman and others that there is nothing in the form or the detailed structure of the text of the *Cathach* that would argue against a date of origin before 600.

It is hoped that further research on this important Irish manuscript, now made available by computer technology for scrutiny by scholars in all relevant disciplines throughout the world, will continue to clarify and enhance our understanding and appreciation of its textual and cultural context.

References

Abbreviated references

AFM O'Donovan, J. (ed.) 1856 *Annála Ríoghachta Éireann. Annals of the Kingdom of Ireland, by the Four Masters, from the earliest period to the year 1616* (2nd edn). Dublin. Hodges, Smith and Co.

AI Mac Airt, S. (ed.) 1951 *The Annals of Inisfallen*. Dublin. Dublin Institute for Advanced Studies.

AU Mac Airt, S. and Mac Niocaill, G. (eds) 1983 *The Annals of Ulster (to AD 1131)*. Dublin. Dublin Institute for Advanced Studies.

AT Stokes, W. (ed.) 1895–7 The Annals of Tigernach. *Revue Celtique* **16**, 374–419; **17**, 6–33, 119–263, 337–420; **18**, 9–59, 150–197, 267–303 (facsimile reprint Felinfach: Llanerch Publishers, 1993).

CLA1 Lowe, E.A. 1935 *Codices Latini antiquiores, Part II: Great Britain and Ireland* (1st edn). Oxford. Clarendon Press.

CLA2 Lowe, E.A. 1972 *Codices Latini antiquiores, Part II: Great Britain and Ireland* (2nd edn). Oxford. Clarendon Press.

OSL *Ordnance Survey Letters, Mayo, vol. 1, 1838*. (MS in Royal Irish Academy.)

PG Migne, J.P. 1857–66 *Patrologia Graeca*, vols 1–161. Paris. The author.

Full references

Alexander, J.J.G. 1978 *Insular manuscripts from the 6th to the 9th century*. London. Harvey Miller.

Anderson, A.O. and Anderson, M.O. 1961 *Adomnan's Life of Columba*. London and Edinburgh. Nelson.

Anderson, M.O. 1991 *Adomnan's Life of Columba*. Oxford. Clarendon Press (revised edn of Anderson and Anderson 1961).

Armstrong, E.C.R. 1916 The Shrine of the Cathach (Appendix I of H.J. Lawlor, The Cathach of St Columba). *Proceedings of the Royal Irish Academy* **33**C (1916–17), 390–6.

Armstrong, E.C.R. and Lawlor, H.J. 1918 *Proceedings of the Royal Irish Academy* **34**, 96–126.

Arnaud-Lindet, M.-P. (ed.) 1990 *Orose, histoires (contre les Païens)*, Tome I, Livres I–III. Paris. Les Belles Lettres.

Badawy, Alexander 1978 *Coptic art and archaeology*. Cambridge, Mass. MIT Press.

Best, R.I. and O'Brien, M.A. 1967 *The Book of Leinster*. Dublin. Dublin Institute for Advanced Studies.

Betham, W. 1826 *Irish antiquarian researches,* Part 1. Dublin. William Curry, Jun. and Co., and Hodges and MacArthur.

Bieler, L. 1963 *Ireland, harbinger of the Middle Ages*. London. Oxford University Press.

Bober, H. 1967 On the illumination of the Glazier Codex, a contribution to early Coptic art and its relation to Hiberno-Saxon interlace. In H. Lehmann-Haupt (ed.), *Homage to a bookman: essays on manuscripts, books and printing written for Hans P. Kraus on his 60th birthday, Oct. 12, 1967*, 31–49. Berlin. Gebr. Mann Verlag.

Breen, A. 1992 The liturgical materials in MS Oxford, Bodleian Library, Auct. F.4./32. *Archiv für Liturgiewissenschaft* **34**, 121–53.

Campbell, J.L. 1986 *Canna: the story of a Hebridean island*. Oxford. Oxford University Press.

Carney, J. 1964 *The poems of Blathmac*. London. Irish Texts Society.

Clancy, T.O. and Márkus, G. 1995 *Iona: the earliest poetry of a Celtic monastery*. Edinburgh. Edinburgh University Press.

Colgan, J. 1647 *Triadis thaumaturgae seu divorum Patricii, Columbae et Brigida…Acta*. Louvain. Cornelius Coenestenius.

Cuppage, J. *et al*. 1986 *Archaeological survey of the Dingle Peninsula. Suirbhé seandálaíochta Chorca Dhuibhne*. Ballyferriter. Oidhreacht Chorca Dhuibhne.

Dinneen. P. (ed.) 1908 *The history of Ireland by Geoffrey Keating, D.D*. London. Irish Texts Society.

Duignan, L. 1973 A hand-pin from Treanmacmurtagh Bog, Co. Sligo. *Journal of the Royal Society of Antiquaries of Ireland* **103**, 220–23.

Duval, P.-M. 1977 *Les Celtes*. Lyons. Gallimard.

Dyer, J. 1989 Monastic psalmody of the Middle Ages. *Revue Benedictine* **99**, 41–74.

Fischer, B. 1952 Die Lesungen der römischen Ostervigil unter Gregor dem Großen. In B. Fischer and V. Fiala (eds), *Colligere fragmenta: Festschrift für Alban Dold*, 144–59. Beuren in Hohenzollern. Erzabtei Beuren.

Fulford, M.G. 1989 Byzantium and Britain: a Mediterranean perspective of post-Roman Mediterranean imports in western Britain and Ireland. *Medieval Archaeology* **33**, 1–6.

Gillespie, F. 1995 Gaelic families of County Donegal. In W. Nolan, L. Ronayne and M. Dunlevy (eds), *Donegal history and society*, 759–838. Templeogue. Geography Publications.

Haseloff, G. 1990 *Email im frühen Mittelalter*. Marburg. Hitzeroth.

Hayes, R. 1949 *Biographical dictionary of Irishmen in France*. Dublin. M.H. Gill.

Heine, R.F. 1995 *Gregory of Nyssa's treatise on the inscriptions of the Psalms*. Oxford. Clarendon Press.

Henderson, G. 1987 *From Durrow to Kells*. London. Thames and Hudson.

Hennessy, W.M. and Kelly, D.H. 1875 *The Book of Fenagh*. Dublin. Alexander Thom.

Henry, F. 1945 Remains of the early Christian period on Inishkea North, Co. Mayo. *Journal of the Royal Society of Antiquaries of Ireland* **75**, 127–55.

Henry, F. 1950 Les débuts de la miniature irlandaise. Gazette des Beaux-Arts **37**, 5–34.

Henry, F. 1951 New monuments from Inishkea North, Co. Mayo. *Journal of the Royal Society of Antiquaries of Ireland* **81**, 65–9.

Henry, F. 1965 *Irish art in the early Christian period (to 800 A.D.).* London. Methuen.

Herbert, M. 1988 *Iona, Kells and Derry: the history and hagiography of the monastic familia of Columba.* Dublin. Four Courts Press (repr. 1996).

Herity, M. 1989 The antiquity of An Turas (The Pilgrimage Round) in Ireland. In A. Lehner and W. Berschin (eds), *Lateinische Kultur im VIII. Jahrhundert,* 95–143. St. Ottilien. E.O.S. Verlag.

Herity, M. 1995a Two island hermitages in the Atlantic: Rathlin O'Birne, Donegal, and Caher Island, Mayo. *Journal of the Royal Society of Antiquaries of Ireland* **125**, 85–128.

Herity, M. 1995b The Chi-Rho and other early cross-forms in Ireland. In J.-M. Picard (ed.), *Aquitaine and Ireland in the Middle Ages*, 233–60. Dublin. Four Courts Press.

Herity, M. 2000 The return of the Cathach to Ireland. In A.P. Smith (ed.), *Seanchas: essays in early medieval archaeology, history and literature in honour of Francis J. Byrne*, 454–64. Dublin. Four Courts Press.

Historical Manuscripts Commission 1902 Calendar of the Stuart Papers. London. HMSO.

Hunt, R.W. 1961 *Saint Dunstan's classbook from Glastonbury: Codex Biblioth. Bodleianae Oxon. Auct. F.4./32.* Amsterdam. North Holland Publishing Company.

Lacey, B. 1998 *Manus O'Donnell: the Life of Colum Cille.* Dublin. Four Courts Press.

Lacy, B. *et al.* 1983 *Archaeological survey of County Donegal.* Lifford. Donegal County Council.

Lapidge, M. 1983 Latin learning in Dark Age Wales: some prolegomena. In D. Ellis Evans (ed.), *Proceedings of the seventh international congress of Celtic studies, held at Oxford, 10–15 July 1983*, 91–107. Oxford. D. Ellis Evans.

Lawlor, H.J. 1916 The Cathach of St Columba. *Proceedings of the Royal Irish Academy* **33** (1916–17), 241–443.

Linton, O. 1961 The interpretation of the Psalms in the early Christian church. *Studia Patristica* **4**, 143–56.

Macalister, R.A.S. 1945 *Corpus inscriptionum insularum Celticarum.* Volume I. Dublin. Stationery Office.

Macalister, R.A.S. 1949 *Corpus inscriptionum insularum Celticarum.* Volume II. Dublin. Stationery Office.

Mc Carthy, Dan 2001 'The chronology of Saint Colum Cille', paper presented at Tionól 2001, 23–4 November 2001, School of Celtic Studies, Dublin Institute for Advanced Studies. The paper was accessed at www.celt.dias.ie/english/tionol/ tionol01.html on 14 December 2001.

McDonough, J. 1962 *Gregorii Nysseni: Inscriptiones in Psalmorum; In sextum Psalmum; In Ecclesiasten.* Leiden. Brill.

Mac Niocaill, G. 1990 The Irish 'Charters'. In P. Fox (ed.), *The Book of Kells, MS 58, Trinity College Library, Dublin: commentary*, 153–65. Luzern. Fine Art Facsimile Publishers of Switzerland / Facsimile Verlag.

McNamara, M. 1973 *Psalter text and Psalter study in the early Irish church* (A.D. 600–1200). *Proceedings of the Royal Irish Academy* **73**C, 201–98.

McNamara, M. 1998 Some affiliations of the St Columba series of Psalm headings: a preliminary study (Part 1). *Proceedings of the Irish Biblical Association* **21**, 87–111.

McNamara, M. 1999 Some affiliations of the St Columba series of Psalm headings: a preliminary study (Part 2). *Proceedings of the Irish Biblical Association* **22**. 91–123. (Repr., with Part 1, in 2000 in M. McNamara, *The Psalms in the early Irish Church*. Sheffield. Sheffield Academic Press.)

Nic Dhonnchadha, L. 1964 *Aided Muirchertaigh Meic Erca.* Dublin. Dublin Institute for Advanced Studies.

Nordenfalk, C. 1947 Before the Book of Durrow. *Acta Archaeologica* **18**, 141–74.

Ó Cochláin, R.S. 1968 The Cathach, battle book of the O'Donnells. *The Irish Sword* **8**, 157–77.

O'Curry, E. 1861 *Lectures on the manuscript materials of ancient Irish history.* Dublin. James Duffy.

Ó Floinn, R. 1995 Sandhills, silver and shrines: fine metalwork of the medieval period from Donegal. In W. Nolan, L. Ronayne and M. Dunlevy (eds), *Donegal history and society*, 85–148. Templeogue: Geography Publications.

O'Kelleher, A. and Schoepperle, G. 1918 *Betha Colaim Chille, Life of Columcille. Compiled by Manus O'Donnell in 1532.* Illinois. University of Illinois. (Repr. 1994 by Dublin Institute for Advanced Studies.)

Ó Riain, P. 1985 *Corpus genealogiarum sanctorum Hiberniae.* Dublin. Dublin Institute for Advanced Studies.

Pächt, O. 1986 *Book illumination in the Middle Ages: an introduction.* London. Harvey Miller and Oxford University Press.

Penna, A. 1959 I titoli del Salterio siriaco e S. Gerolamo. *Biblica* **40**, 177–87.

Plummer, Charles 1910 *Vitae sanctorum Hiberniae.* 2 vols. Oxford. Clarendon Press.

Raftery, B. 1983 *A catalogue of Irish Iron Age antiquities.* Marburg. Veröffentlichung des Vorgeschichtlichen Seminars Marburg.

Rahlfs, A. 1979 *Psalmi cum Odis. Septuaginta Vetus Testamentum Graecum X* (3rd edn). Göttingen. Vandenhoeck & Ruprecht.

Ralegh Radford, C.A. 1956 Imported pottery found at Tintagel, Cornwall. In D.B. Harden (ed.) *Dark-Age Britain*, 59–70. London. Methuen.

Reeves, W. 1857 *The Life of St Columba*. Dublin. The Irish Archaeological and Celtic Society.

Richardson, H. 1987 Observations on Christian art in early Ireland, Georgia and Armenia. In M. Ryan (ed.), *Ireland and insular Art, AD 500–1200*, 129–37. Dublin. Royal Irish Academy (repr. 2002).

Rondeau, M.-J. 1958 Une nouvelle preuve de l'influence d'Eusèbe de Césarée sur Athanase: l'interprétation des Psaumes. *Recherches de Science Religieuse* **56**, 385–434.

Roth, U. 1979 Studien zur Ornamentik frühchristlicher Handschriften des insularen Bereichs von den Anfängen bis zum Book of Durrow. *Bericht der Römisch-Germanischen Kommission* **60**, 7–225.

Salmon, Pierre 1959 *Les 'Tituli Psalmorum' des manuscrits latins (Collectanea Biblica Latina XII)*. Rome. Vatican.

Salmon, Pierre 1962 *The breviary through the centuries*. Collegeville, Minnesota. Liturgical Press.

Schauman, B.T. 1978 The Irish script of the MS Milan, Biblioteca Ambrosiana, S. 45 sup. (ante ca. 625). *Scriptorium* **32**, 3–18.

Sharpe, R. 1995 *Adomnán of Iona: Life of St Columba*. Harmondsworth. Penguin.

Smyth, A.P. 1984 *Warlords and holy men, Scotland AD 80–1000*. London. Edward Arnold.

Thomas, A.C. 1959 Imported pottery in Dark Age western Britain. *Medieval Archaeology* **3**, 89–111.

Thomas, A.C. 1981 *A provisional list of imported pottery in post-Roman western Britain and Ireland*. Redruth. Institute of Cornish Studies.

Vian, G.M. 1991 Il *De Psalmorum titulis*: il esegesi di Attanasio tra Eusebio e Cirillo. *Orpheus* **12**, 93–132.

Wilde, W.R. 1861 *A descriptive catalogue of the antiquities of animal materials and bronze in the museum of the Royal Irish Academy*. Dublin. Hodges, Smith and Co.

Wilde, W.R. 1867 *Lough Corrib, its shores and islands*. Dublin. McGlashan and Gill.

Williams, N.J.A. 1980 *Poems of Giolla Brighde mac Con Midhe*. London. Irish Texts Society.

Woolfenden, G.W. 1993 The use of the Psalter by early monastic communities. *Studia Patristica* **26**, 88–94.

Appendix 1

Irish placenames mentioned in the *Cathach* booklet, pp 1–60

Placename	County
Armagh	Armagh
Assaroe	Donegal
Ballymagrorty	Donegal
Ballyshannon	Donegal
Bealach Buidhe	Roscommon
Bangor	Down
Boyle	Roscommon
Caher Island	Mayo
Clonamery	Kilkenny
Clonmacnoise	Offaly
Cong	Mayo
Conwal	Donegal
Cúl Drebene (Cooldrumman)	Sligo
Derry	Londonderry
Devenish Island	Fermanagh
Dromsnat	Monaghan
Drumcliff	Sligo
Drumhome	Donegal
Dulane	Meath
Durrow	Offaly
Elphin	Roscommon
Fearsad Mór	Donegal
Fenagh	Leitrim
Gartan	Donegal
Glasnevin	Dublin
Glend Colaim Cilli (Gleann Choluim Cille / Glencolmcille)	Donegal
Glendalough	Wicklow
Illauntannig	Kerry
Inishkea Islands	Mayo
Kells	Meath
Killeen	Mayo
Kilmacrenan	Donegal
Kilmore	Cavan
Kilshannig	Kerry
Kilvickadownig	Kerry

Knockane	Kerry
Lambay	Dublin
Letterkenny	Donegal
Lifford	Donegal
Loch Beagh	Donegal
Maumanorig	Kerry
Moone	Kildare
Moville	Down
Moylurg	Roscommon
Nendrum	Down
Newport	Mayo
Racoon	Donegal
Ramelton	Donegal
Rathlin O'Birne Island	Donegal
Swords	Dublin
Tara	Meath
Treanmacmurtagh Bog	Sligo

Appendix 2

Pages 7–10 (reproduction at 60% of original) of 'Report on the repair and rebinding of the *Cathach* together with further notes and observations' by Roger Powell († 1990)

It is clear that Lawlor was not conversant with the practice of Irish and other Insular scribes in preparing vellum leaves for writing. What follows is put forward in the light of experience in dealing with many Insular manuscript books from Trinity College, Dublin, The Royal Irish Academy and elsewhere including The Book of Durrow, The Book of Armagh, The Lichfield St. Chad Gospels, A.II.27 from Durham, The Book of Kells and in examining The Stonyhurst Gospel of St. John for "The Relics of St. Cuthbert", Durham Cathedral and "The Stonyhurst Gospel of St. John", the Roxburghe Club.

In attempting to establish the original quiring of The Cathach of St. Columba the starting point is the tendency for Irish and Irish-inspired mss. to be arranged in 10-leaf quires, usually of 5 conjoint bifolia. Applying this to The Cathach, on ff.9, 19, 29, 39 and 49 the pricking for ruling (meticulously on the vertical rules) and especially the ruling (meticulously confined within the vertical rules) is markedly heavier than on the following nine leaves where it gradually fades away. This shows that both pricking and ruling was performed from the top leaf of each assembled quire and that there was no re-ruling of the lower leaves. That there is now no trace of ruling on the lower leaves does not mean that there were no impressions when it was ruled; the damp conditions over hundreds of years and the immersion by Betham when separating the leaves allowed recovery. The fact that re-ruling was not always necessary, though often practised in later ms., is an interesting comment on the different character of early vellum compared with what is available today.

Comparing the hair and flesh sides of the quiring suggested

by the pricking and ruling from f.9 to the end shows that except
for single leaves at ff.10 and 17 and ff.21 and 26 the remainder
was made up of 23 conjoint bifolia, so confirming the 10-leaf
quiring, and in turn suggesting that ff.1 - 8 are what remains
of a 10-leaf quire of which the first two leaves (now missing)
were conjoint with ff.8 and 7 and having hair-sides on verso and
recto respectively. Within the quire the arrangement of hair and
flesh sides is indiscrimminate with a slight tendency for flesh-
sides to be outwards.

        There is some evidence that while the ms. was in single
leaves it was stabbed (in quires?), perhaps with a thread passing
through one, two and possibly three widely separated holes. These
holes appear in or near the inner margins near the head and equi-
distant from head and tail. The middle one is clearly vissible
from f.3 - f.28. One near the head is visible from f.8 - f.28.
Two further series only visible at the head seem to run from f.29 -
f.38 and from f.39 - f.48.

        An area of pricked(?) holes in the middle of f.58 penetrates
decreasingly through the preceding leaves; one, undoubtedly a
piercing, persists through to f.32.

Roger Powell.

Key for diagram overleaf:-

⊙	Red dots in manuscript, recto or verso indicated.
◪	Other colour on initials, recto or verso indicated.
△	Small hole pierced half-way up inner edge of folio.
⊙	Folio pierced at inner head, green stain begins the run.
⊡	Folio pierced at centre, green stain.
⑤	Folio pierced at centre head, rusty stain.
⊛	Folio pierced over central area up to fifteen times.

PROBABLE GATHERINGS	HAIR SIDE				
Folio 1	R	Reversed in replacement.			
2	R	Folio 3 previously, reversed in replacement.			
3	R	Folio 2 previously, reversed in replacement.			△
4	V				△
5	V				△
6	V				△
7	V		☼ V		△
8	R		☼ V		△
9	V				◉ △
10	R				◉ △
11	V		☼ RV		◉ △
12	R	Reversed in replacement.		☑ V	◉ △
13	V				◉ △
14	R		☼ RV	☑ RV	◉ △
15	V		☼ V	☑ V	◉ △
16	R				◉ △
17	R		☼ V	☑ V	◉ △
18	R		☼ V	☑ V	◉ △
19	V		☼ R	☑ R	◉ △
20	V		☼ V		◉ △
21	V		☼ RV	☑ RV	◑ △
22	V		☼ V	☑ R	◑ △
23	V		☼ RV	☑ RV	◑ △
24	R		☼ V		◑ △
25	R		☼ R	☑ R	◑ △
26	V				◑ △
27	R				◑ △
28	R		☼ V		◑

10

PROBABLE GATHERINGS	Folio	HAIR SIDE						
	29	V					⊘	
	30	V		◌V	☑V		⊘	
	31	V		◌V	☑V		⊘	
	32	V		◌V	☑V		⊘	
	33	V		◌V			⊘	
	34	R		◌V	☑V		⊘	☐
	35	R	Folio 36 previously.	◌RV	☑V		⊘	☐
	36	R	Folio 35 previously.	◌V	☑V		⊘	☐
	37	R					⊘	☐
	38	R					⊘	☐
	39	R		◌V	☑V			☐
	40	V		◌R	☑R			☐
	41	V		◌RV	☑RV			☐
	42	V	Folio 43 previously.					☐
	43	R	Folio 42 previously.		☑V		⑥	☐
	44	V			☑V	⊘	⑥	☐
	45	R				⊘	⑥	☐
	46	R				⊘	⑥	☐
	47	R				⊘	⑥	☐
	48	V				⊘	⑥	☐
	49	R				⊘	⑥	☐
	50	V				⊘	⑥	☐
	51	V				⊘	⑥	☐
	52	V				⊘	⑥	☐
	53	R				⊘		☐
	54	V				⊘		☐
	55	R				⊘		☐
	56	R				⊘		☐
	57	R				⊘		☐
	58	V				⊘		☐

Appendix 3
The Springmount Bog wax tablets

The following is an extract from a paper by Martin McNamara on 'Psalter text and psalter study in the early Irish Church (AD 600–1200), published in *Proceedings of the Royal Irish Academy* 73C (1973), 201–98, and updated by Fr McNamara in 2001–2002 for this publication. It also includes extracts from the late Dr Maurice Sheehy's Appendix to the above paper, pp 277–80, and his reading of the text on fol. 3v of the tablets.

These tablets were found in Springmount Bog, about half a mile from the village of Clough, Co. Antrim, and seven miles north of Ballymena. They were purchased by the National Museum of Ireland in 1914 from Mr W. Gregg of Clough. The tablets probably come from an ancient monastery.

They consist of a book of six wooden 'leaves', inlaid with wax on both sides of each (except the two outer ones, which have no wax on the outside). The six tablets when found were bound together as a book by a thong of leather stitching which passed through the holes perforating one edge of the tablets, thus forming a loose spine; two bands of leather were placed around the book, at the top and the bottom. The tablets measure approximately 21cm by 7.7cm and each is 6 to 7mm thick.

The tablets contain the text of Psalms 30–32 (in the Vulgate numbering). The text is Gallican, with some readings due to the influence of the Old Latin and others arising, it would appear, from carelessness in transcription or from the fact that the writer depended on his memory.

The tablets were probably used in primary instruction, to initiate a pupil into the arts of reading and writing through the psalter, or Book of Psalms, as was the custom. The scribe in this instance was probably the schoolmaster. The purpose of the tablets probably explains the inaccuracies of transcription.

The original editors, Armstrong and Macalister (1920) made no attempt to date the tablets. Dr Bernhard Bischoff, in a letter to J.N. Hillgarth (Hillgarth 1962, 183), noted that the script of the tablets has the same cursive characteristics as the fragments of Isidore in MS St. Gall 1399 a. 1 (seventh century) and Codex Usserianus Primus (Trinity College, Dublin, 55; beginning of seventh century), both of which are in Irish script. The tablets would thus be of a seventh-century date. In a more detailed study, D.H. Wright (1963) dates them to about AD 600.

Since Wright's contribution, studies on the palaeography of the tablets have been made by B. Schauman (1974, 308–10; 1979, 35–7) in particular but also by T. Julian Brown (1982, 104; 1984, 312, 320, 321) and W. O'Sullivan (1994, 177–9). With regard to the date to be assigned to them, Bischoff (1990, 14 n. 43), with reference to Wright (1963, 219), says that they may be dated around AD 600. According to Schauman (1979, 37) the archaic features of the script argue against a date as late as the seventh century and in favour of a rather early date for the tablets. In her opinion it is not unreasonable to place them in the sixth century; indeed, she believes they may well represent a type of hand common in Ireland as early as St Patrick's day. In T. Julian Brown's (1982, 104) opinion the tablets cannot be dated by internal evidence, and it is perhaps enough to ascribe them to the first half of the seventh century. David Dumville (1999, 31–5) reviews the various opinions put forward with regard to the script and date of the tablets. Despite Bischoff's rejection of the likelihood of an import from Bobbio (Bischoff in Hillgarth 1962, 183 n. 78), Dumville (1999, 35) remarks that while it might seem simpler to rule any scribe from abroad out of consideration, it is not absolutely to be excluded that these tablets were written in the context of sixth- (or fifth-) century British missionary endeavour in Ireland.

Despite this observation, the almost unanimous scholarly opinion is that in these tablets we have one of the oldest extant specimens of Irish writing. The tablets also provide precious evidence that even at this early date pupils were being initiated into the arts of reading and writing through the Gallican text of the psalter, not through the Old Latin. And, in fact, it is the Gallican text, and it alone, that we shall find as the biblical text used in all later Irish commentaries.

Folio 3v of the tablets (below) represents Psalm 31:1–7a. <Angle brackets> indicate missing or illegible text, [square brackets] indicate editorial emendation.

Folio 3v of the Springmount Bog wax tablets. (© National Museum of Ireland

Column 1
<Beati, quoru>m remisse sunt iniquitates
<et quoru>m tecta sunt peccata.
<Beat>us vir cui non inpotavit Dominus peccatum,
<n>ec est in spiritu eius dolos. Quoniam t<a>cui in-
<ve>teraverunt in me ossa mea d<um cla>ma-
rem tota die. Quoniam die ac nocte
gravata est super me m<anu>s t<u>a,
conversus sum in er<?>omna mea,
dum configitur mihi spina.

Column 2
Dilictum meum cognitum tibi fe<ci>
et iniustiam meam non absco<ndi>.
Dixi: confitebor adversus me [iniustitiam meam Domino] et <tu>
rimisisti impietatem peccati mei.
Pro hac orabit ad te omnis sanctis in
tempore oportuno,
verumtamen in diluvio aquarum
multarum ad [eu]m non proximabunt.
Tu es refugium meum